FOOTBALL ⚫ SUPERSTARS

Joe Montana

FOOTBALL SUPERSTARS

Tiki Barber

Tom Brady

John Elway

Brett Favre

Peyton Manning

Dan Marino

Donovan McNabb

Joe Montana

Walter Payton

Jerry Rice

Ben Roethlisberger

Barry Sanders

FOOTBALL ● SUPERSTARS

Joe
Montana

Adam Woog

CHELSEA HOUSE
PUBLISHERS
An imprint of Infobase Publishing

My thanks to Tom DeGraff for his generous gifts
of time and expertise. —A.W.

JOE MONTANA

Copyright © 2008 by Infobase Publishing

Chelsea House
An imprint of Infobase Publishing
132 West 31st Street
New York NY 10001

Library of Congress Cataloging-in-Publication Data
Woog, Adam, 1953-
 Joe Montana / Adam Woog.
     p. cm. — (Football superstars)
 Includes bibliographical references and index.
 ISBN 978-0-7910-9568-3 (hardcover)
 1. Montana, Joe, 1956—Juvenile literature. 2. Football players—United States—
Biography—Juvenile literature. I. Title. II. Series.

 GV939.M59W66 2008
 796.332092—dc22
 [B]
                                 2008005714

Chelsea House books are available at special discounts when purchased in bulk quantities
for businesses, associations, institutions, or sales promotions. Please call our Special Sales
Department in New York at (212) 967-8800 or (800) 322-8755.

You can find Chelsea House on the World Wide Web at http://www.chelseahouse.com

Text design by Erik Lindstrom
Cover design by Ben Peterson

Printed in the United States of America

Bang EJB 10 9 8 7 6 5 4 3 2 1

This book is printed on acid-free paper.

All links and Web addresses were checked and verified to be correct at the time
of publication. Because of the dynamic nature of the Web, some addresses and links
may have changed since publication and may no longer be valid.

CONTENTS

Meet Joe Cool

It is difficult to pick out a single moment that defines an outstanding athlete's career. Out of a lifetime filled with high points, choosing the best is, at best, a risky proposition. Sometimes, though, one single event summarizes everything that is great about an athlete. For Joe Montana, considered by many to be the greatest **quarterback** in football history, that time may have been in the closing minutes of the **National Football Conference** (NFC) Championship Game on January 10, 1982.

The contest, which was held at Candlestick Park in San Francisco, pitted Montana's team, the San Francisco 49ers, against the heavily favored Dallas Cowboys. The stakes were high: If the Niners won the battle, they would go on to make their first-ever Super Bowl appearance after a long period of mediocre seasons.

The underdog 49ers had played well, with the score seesawing repeatedly in favor of one team or the other. Nonetheless, as the contest entered its closing minutes, the 49ers were lagging behind. In fact, it seemed to be an impossible situation.

San Francisco was down 27-21 and on its own 11-**yard** line. A mere 4:54 was left in the game. The state of affairs was starkly clear: The 49ers had to travel 89 yards in less than five minutes, clashing at every step with a formidable opponent, if they wanted to get a shot at playing in the Super Bowl.

So Joe Montana went to work.

Calm and cool, in command of his team despite the tremendous pressure, he led San Francisco on a heroic march up the field. By the time 58 seconds were left on the clock, the 49ers had reached the Cowboys' 6-yard line, third and three. That was impressive enough, though of course it was not sufficient to win the game. But then came one of the most famous plays in National Football League history, a play so outstanding that it was given its own name: It is known to fans simply as "The Catch."

The play was supposed to be a pass to **wide receiver** Freddie Solomon; earlier in the game, Montana and Solomon had scored a **touchdown** on the same maneuver. But Solomon, Montana's primary receiver, was well covered. The quarterback instead relied on his secondary receiver, Dwight Clark. He threw a high pass to Clark in the back of the **end zone**, and Clark caught it with his fingertips. The game was now tied with 51 seconds left; the 49ers kicked the **extra point** and went on to win the game.

JOE COOL

The spectacular last five minutes of that game proved to be a defining moment in Montana's life and career. Beforehand, he was reasonably well known but hardly a household name; afterward, he was a legend. Those few minutes of play

Dwight Clark, a receiver with the San Francisco 49ers, leaped high in the end zone to catch a pass from quarterback Joe Montana in the final minute of the National Football Conference Championship Game on January 10, 1982. The play has become so legendary that it is simply known by fans as "The Catch." The score completed an 89-yard drive led by Montana that lifted the 49ers over the Dallas Cowboys 28-27.

also perfectly summed up Montana's gifts as an athlete, demonstrating the truth behind his two famous nicknames.

One nickname was "Joe Cool." Montana was affectionately called this because of his remarkable calm in the face of the worst chaos or the toughest odds. Even when the pressure was so strong that his teammates were close to panic, Joe Cool stayed focused and tranquil—and equally important, he was able to focus his team around him.

This gift let Montana handle even crucial moments—like the pressure-cooker final seconds of a closely fought game—as if they were just any ordinary period in any ordinary game. Bill Walsh, the 49ers coach, once remarked in *Sports Illustrated*, "He's got this resourcefulness, this something that's hard to put into words. He won't choke. Or rather, if he ever does, you'll know everyone else has come apart first."

Montana also had a quiet sense of self-confidence; when he was in the zone, he was sure that he would prevail. He just knew it. Montana has remarked that, when all facets of the game were flowing well for him and he had sufficient time to throw, he simply could not be stopped. This feeling was tremendously liberating, and the results were astonishing; *Sports Illustrated* writer Leigh Montville pointed out, "The unflappability that sets him free is almost eerie."

"THE ONLY GUY TO GET"

Montana's cool also let him see the big picture. It has often been said that Montana remained unruffled because he appeared to see the game in slow motion. This perception let him instantly assess a situation, react intelligently to it, and find a way to get through it. He saw order and opportunity where others saw only chaos and danger. Dwight Clark said in the *San Francisco Chronicle*, "He knew where everybody was on the field. His field vision, I think, is what set him apart from a lot of people. He knew where to go on his pre-snap read. And if he got fooled, he could react quickly and still make the right read."

But Joe Cool was not Montana's only nickname. He was also called "The Comeback Kid." This was in recognition of his uncanny ability, dating from his earliest days as a football player, to rally a trailing team in the fourth quarter of a game, turning his teammates into a single, focused unit and leading them to victory.

Time and again, The Comeback Kid quarterbacked a fourth-quarter, come-from-behind triumph. Time and again, he pulled off a seemingly impossible magic trick. Sportswriter Rick Reilly called this ability—Montana's knack for turning seeming disaster into victory at the last minute—the "impossible, get-serious, did-you-hear-what-happened-after-we-left comeback."

Because of this gift, Montana became the one guy that any team would really want and need most when the heat was on. His longtime teammate, 49ers **offensive lineman** Randy Cross, said in an article on ESPN.com, "There have been, and will be, much better arms and legs and much better bodies on quarterbacks in the NFL, but if you have to win a game or score a touchdown or win a championship, the only guy to get is Joe Montana."

STAR QUALITIES

As Cross pointed out, Montana was not unusually tall or heavy or fast, and he did not have the rocket-powered throwing arm of other quarterbacks. But, it goes without saying, he was an excellent athlete, and he combined this natural athleticism with many other good qualities: brains, grace, reliability, toughness—and that eerie calmness. Furthermore, he could withstand and play through pain, he was brilliant at reading his opponents' defenses, and he could keep an eye on every aspect of the field at once.

Together, these qualities gave Montana a stellar career—first as a high school player in small-town Pennsylvania, then for the University of Notre Dame's famous Fighting Irish, then during a long career with San Francisco, and finally through his last years with the Kansas City Chiefs.

Most of Montana's playing years, his years of glory, were with the Niners. This was his peak period, when he seemed unstoppable. During those years, commented sportswriter Dave Anderson in *The New York Times*, "No quarterback has ever been tougher, physically or mentally." And he was still a formidable athlete during his final two years in Kansas City.

KILLER STATISTICS

Taken together, Montana's career was a remarkable one. Counting his time with both the Niners and the Chiefs—a total of 16 years in the NFL—Montana directed his teams to 31 come-from-behind wins in the fourth quarter. He won more than 70 percent of the games he started in his pro career, and he led his teams to the playoffs 12 times. Montana's team won all four Super Bowls in which he played. He is the only player to earn the Super Bowl's Most Valuable Player (MVP) award three times and the only one to be a two-time NFL MVP.

Montana completed 3,409 out of 5,391 passes, for 40,551 yards with 273 touchdowns and 139 **interceptions**. In the 23 postseason games he played, he completed 460 of 734 passes for 5,772 yards, with 45 touchdowns and 21 interceptions. These numbers place Montana among the top 10 quarterbacks in the history of the NFL in passes attempted, passes completed, passing yardage, and touchdown passes.

The numbers and records alone are impressive enough, but what is even more amazing is that Montana made it all seem simple. He made impossible plays look easy. He made a brutal, nerve-wracking, dangerous job—being a starting quarterback in the NFL—look easy. He even made winning the Super Bowl look easy.

Of course, this was an illusion—part of Montana's magic. Tough situations just made Montana work at top capacity. Writer Dick Schaap commented, "It would be unfair, and

Joe Montana avoided the Dolphins' rush to get off a pass during Super Bowl XIX on January 20, 1985, in Stanford Stadium. Montana was named the Most Valuable Player of that year's Super Bowl   one of a record three times that he was voted the Super Bowl MVP.

inaccurate, to say that Joe Montana was not affected by pressure. He was. Under pressure, he played better."

THE PUBLIC FACE OF THE 49ERS

Montana's career with the Niners more or less coincided with the team's years of glory. The history of pro football can often be roughly divided into periods during which certain teams dominated the sport. For example, in the 1960s the Green Bay Packers ruled the roost. They won five NFL championships in seven years, a feat unmatched by any other team.

In the early '70s, it was the Miami Dolphins—the first NFL team to appear in three consecutive Super Bowls, the second team ever to win back-to-back championships, and the only NFL team to go a full season undefeated and untied. In the mid- to late 1970s, the Pittsburgh Steelers took over as the dominant team, racking up four Super Bowl wins in four appearances—the first NFL team to do so.

The 49ers were the top dogs in pro football in the 1980s. During those years, San Francisco won all four of its Super Bowl appearances, tying the Steelers' previous record. And a significant reason for San Francisco's dominance during the decade was the presence of Joe Montana.

His **rookie** year in San Francisco was 1979. Almost immediately he began to dominate the team, and the team in turn

"HE WAS JOE COOL"

In this passage from the book *Montana*, writer Dick Schaap summarizes just some of the accomplishments of the man whom many consider to be the greatest quarterback of all time:

He was Joe Cool, the quarterback who never quit, the quarterback who could overcome any deficit, any pressure, any injury.

Once, Joe Montana led his team to victory after trailing by twenty-eight points at halftime.

More than once, Montana led his team to victory after trailing by fourteen points in the fourth quarter.

Thirty-one times, Montana led his team to victory after trailing in the fourth quarter, and more than three-fourths of those trademark comebacks took place on the road, heroics in front of hostile crowds.

Four times in four appearances in the brightest spotlight, Montana led his team to victory in the Super Bowl.

began to dominate the sport. From 1981, Montana's first full season as a starter, through 1990, his last year as a starter, San Francisco finished first in its division every year except for two. (The exceptions were the 1982 strike-shortened season, when division standings were ignored and the 49ers finished eleventh overall in the NFC, and the 1985 season, when they finished in second place.)

San Francisco became the team of the decade—and Montana became the best-known figure associated with the team. His relaxed, friendly persona was the public face of the 49ers—the one person most immediately identified with the team, a regular guy who loved to play football.

THE EASYGOING GENERAL

Whether you were watching from the stands or from a couch in front of a television, Montana made it seem effortless, and off the field he was always laid-back, charming, and even-tempered.

He showed a lack of ego that was remarkable in a professional athlete—not a vocation generally known for quiet, retiring modesty. Montana always put the welfare of the team above his own glory. **Placekicker** Nick Lowery, who played with Montana on the Kansas City Chiefs, remarked, "Most quarterbacks ask, 'What do I have to do to help us win?' Joe asks, 'Who do I have to get the ball to, to help us win?'"

Montana's public manner and general lack of ego, though, masked a steely resolve. This resolve—coupled with a need to control the show and direct the flow of play—was clearly evident to his teammates, especially when they were in the huddle together. Dwight Clark said in the *San Francisco Chronicle*, "The Joe Montana aura is really an amazing thing. Here's a guy who's shy and quiet off the field—a kid, really—but on the field he was like a general. He was running the show, and you always knew it."

Of course, Montana also had a competitive streak as powerful as a freight train. After all, no one becomes an NFL

Reporters and cameramen mobbed Joe Montana during a practice in January 1988 at the 49ers' training camp in Redwood City, California. The Niners were preparing to face the Minnesota Vikings in an NFC playoff game. Montana was the public face of the 49ers— the team's most famous player during its most successful decade.

quarterback without wanting to be the very best at it. Montana, however, was not just competitive about football. According to Clark, his competitiveness popped up everywhere: "He just competed at everything. If it was driving home, it was who was going to get home first. When he played pool or Ping-Pong or video games, it was always a highly competitive situation."

That competitive streak, as might be expected, began long before Montana's career in the pros began. Montana was a gifted natural athlete from early childhood. The story thus starts in the region where Joe grew up: the tough-minded, football-crazy Monongahela Valley of Pennsylvania.

Early Days

The Monongahela Valley in southwest Pennsylvania is a tough, blue-collar part of the country. It has long been associated with heavy industries like coal mining and steel production. Sturdy work like this requires sturdy workers, and the region has long attracted people from a wide variety of tightly knit immigrant and minority groups, including Serbs, Croats, Slavs, Greeks, Russians, African Americans, Poles, and Irish. These various groups differ from each other in many respects, of course, but they also typically share certain characteristics.

They appreciate such virtues as hard work, commitment, and competitiveness. They share an attitude of no-nonsense, get-it-done practicality. And they take their sports seriously—sometimes as seriously as the rest of life. Writer Dick Schaap commented about the Monongahela Valley, "Even pick-up softball games . . . are played for blood, cousins against cousins, brothers against brothers. They play fair, but they play hard, and no one likes to lose."

A BIRTHPLACE OF GREAT QUARTERBACKS

Not surprisingly, therefore, professional and college sports have attracted fanatically loyal followings in the region for generations. Football is perhaps the most avidly followed sport of all. Naturally enough, fans in the Monongahela Valley are especially faithful supporters of local teams like the Pittsburgh Steelers, the University of Pittsburgh, and Penn State.

The Pittsburgh area, though, has not only produced rabid fans. It has also been the home of a surprisingly large number of notable football players—including, for some reason, a number of outstanding quarterbacks. Among the many who grew up in the region and became legendary quarterbacks are Johnny Unitas, Dan Marino, Joe Namath, Johnny Lujack, George Blanda, Jim Kelly, Terry Hanratty . . . and Joe Montana.

Why has this part of the country given birth to so many football greats, especially quarterbacks? According to sportswriter Paul Zimmerman, at least part of the answer lies in the region's roots. The region produced a few greats, and it snowballed: The quarterbacks of years past now serve as idols and role models for the quarterbacks of the future. In *Sports Illustrated*, Zimmerman wrote, "The most logical answer is tradition—and focus. If you're a kid with athletic ability in western Pennsylvania, you've probably got a picture of Montana or Marino on your wall."

AN EARLY LOVE OF SPORTS

Joseph Clifford Montana, Jr.—the man who was, arguably, the greatest quarterback of them all—was born on June 11, 1956, in New Eagle, Pennsylvania. He grew up in the nearby town of Monongahela, 30 miles (48 kilometers) upriver from Pittsburgh.

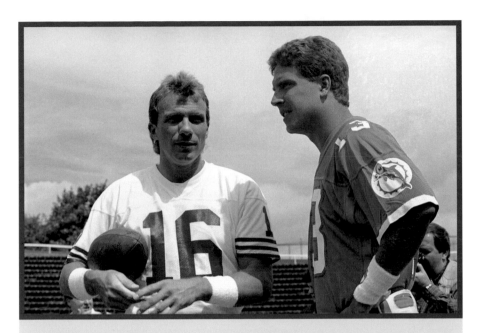

Quarterbacks Joe Montana of the 49ers and Dan Marino of the Miami Dolphins met up during a practice in London, England, in July 1988. Their teams were in Great Britain to play an exhibition game. Montana and Marino both grew up in the Pittsburgh area, which has been the birthplace of many other great quarterbacks, like Johnny Unitas, Jim Kelly, and Joe Namath.

Joey, as he was called, was the only child of Joe Montana, Sr., and Theresa Montana. (Joe is of Italian descent on his father's side; the family name was originally Montani.) The Montana family lived in a modest, two-story frame house at 512 Park Avenue, in a middle-class neighborhood of Monongahela.

When Joey was born, his father was working as a telephone equipment installer. When the boy was three, Joe, Sr., changed jobs. He took a position managing the office of the Civic Finance Company. Joe's mother worked at the same finance company. She handled its accounts.

From a very early age, Joey showed considerable athletic ability. His mother recalled that he used to wreck his crib by standing up and rocking in it. She said in *Sports Illustrated*,

"Then he'd climb up on the side and jump to our bed. You'd hear a thump in the middle of the night and know he hit the bed and went on the floor."

Joe, Sr., saw that his boy was athletic, and he fostered his son's interest in sports as soon as possible and whenever possible. Joey was happy to be encouraged in that direction. As far back as he could remember, playing sports was always the main focus of his life. On the other hand, by his own account, he did not have many other options; according to Montana, there was not much else to do in "Mon City" but play sports. Writer Tom Callahan noted, "There never seems to have been a doubt that Montana would become some sort of ballplayer."

A FAMILY AFFAIR

Joe not only enjoyed sports; he excelled in every one he tried. He loved baseball and basketball, and he organized pickup games with other kids as often as he could. But he was an especially good football player, and he played the game at every opportunity. Whenever he took part in a game, Joe was always the quarterback.

Young Joe was keenly aware of the area's heritage of football greats, and he idolized the standout players the region had produced. Two particular heroes of his were quarterbacks Johnny Unitas, who had an outstanding career with the Baltimore Colts, and Terry Hanratty, who was less well known but also gifted. (Hanratty played for Notre Dame and spent most of his pro career as a backup quarterback for the Steelers in the 1970s.) Joe had other heroes, too, he recalled: "When I wasn't pretending I was [Joe] Namath or [Len] Dawson, I was pretending I was [Terry] Bradshaw."

Joe also knew that he had an athletic family. His grandfather, also named Joe but nicknamed "Hooks," had played minor-league football in the 1920s. The older man watched his grandson play as a young boy, although he apparently kept what he thought about Joe's potential to himself. Montana recalled, "I'm told that my grandfather Joe used to tell my grandmother that I was special, that I was going to be good, but I don't remember him ever telling me."

TOSSING THE BALL AROUND

Meanwhile, Joe's father, Joe, Sr., was an excellent all-around athlete in his own right. As a teenager, Joe, Sr., had been too slim and spare to make any of the high school teams when he was growing up in Monongahela. Later, though, he filled out and made a name for himself in the Navy playing football, basketball, and baseball. He maintained his love of sports for the rest of his life.

The passion that the elder Montana shared with his son ran deep, and he was eager to pass on all that he knew. In Zimmerman's *Sports Illustrated* article, Joe, Sr., recalled, "When I was a kid, I never had anyone to take me in the backyard and throw a ball to me. Maybe that's why I got Joe started in sports. Once he got started, he was always waiting at the door with a ball when I came home from work. . . . He loved it so much, and I loved watching him. And I wanted to make sure he learned the right way."

Almost every day after school, Joe would sit on the steps of their house and wait for his father. The two of them would then spend hours at one game or another, shooting hoops at the net that Joe, Sr., installed on their garage or tossing a football in the alley behind their house.

Often, they went to a neighbor's yard and borrowed a tire swing that was hanging in a tree there for target practice. Joe, Sr., would push the swing back and forth, and his son would try to throw a football through it. This gave young Joe excellent practice in pinpoint throwing accuracy. And Joe loved such practice: He says his fondest childhood memory is of playing ball with his father, then coming into the family's kitchen, where his mother would have a pot of ravioli cooking on the stove.

"I DIDN'T LIKE TO LOSE, EITHER"

Early on, Joe learned that he had to be as intensely competitive as his father if he wanted to succeed. He said of Joe, Sr., "He didn't like to lose. He grabbed. He pushed. He was the kind of guy who would step on your foot if you tried to go around him. Or trip you as you went by. I learned his tricks. I didn't like to lose, either."

When it came to sports, Joe's father wanted to help his son in every way. He was not even above bending the truth a little to help out. Joe, Sr., once lied about his son's age to get him into a Pop Warner peewee football program early. Boys were supposed to be nine years old to enroll, but when Joey was eight, his father fibbed and got him in.

In that program, Joe became one of the top players on his team, the Little Wildcats. Montana recalled that the coach of the Wildcats, Carl Crawley, had excellent "kid skills"—that is, he knew how to talk to his young players and make them understand a concept.

For his part, the coach remembers Joe well. "We ran a pro offense," Crawley said in *Sports Illustrated* during Montana's professional career, "with a lot of the stuff he's doing now, the underneath stuff. Joe would roll out. If the **cornerback** came off, he'd dump it off; if he stayed back, he'd keep going and pick up five or six yards. He was an amazingly accurate passer for a kid."

A LESSON ABOUT NOT QUITTING

Despite his obsession with athletics, Joe nearly gave up at one point. When he was 10, he told his father that he wanted to quit organized sports and join the Cub Scouts instead. He recalled, "My cousins were in the Cub Scouts, and I thought that might be more fun than playing football."

His dad told him that he could quit after the season if he still wanted to but that he had to stay for the rest of the season. It would not have been right, or fair to his teammates, to walk out on something he had already started. Joe understood his father's point about commitment. By the time he finished the season, he had forgotten about his interest in the Scouts. He stuck with sports.

Joe, Sr., was tough on his son and sometimes seemed overbearing, but it was for a reason. "I love my kid, whether he ever played football or not," the elder Montana remarked later in *Time*. "But the part of him that made him so special, I loved that, too. I'd say to him: 'Joey, it's not easy for me to holler at you; it kills me.' Joe understood. He wanted the things for himself that I wanted for him."

BASEBALL AND BASKETBALL, TOO

As he grew, Joe remained hooked on other sports besides football; baseball and basketball remained equally strong interests. He avidly watched them on television, too. Surprisingly, however, as a kid Joe never went to see any games played by the Pittsburgh Steelers or baseball's Pirates. In fact, he never saw a professional football game in person until he played in one himself. He says now that he was just too busy playing ball to go to games as well.

Although Joe always focused on being the quarterback in football, he liked to play every position in basketball and baseball. And he did well at all of them. As a star Little League pitcher, for instance, he had a career that included three perfect games. The only position he disliked in baseball, he claimed, was catcher: "I didn't care much for foul tips," he said in *Time*, "but I could catch and, to my father, not liking something you were good at doing wasn't a good enough reason for not doing it."

He loved basketball, too. Joe, Sr., worked a lot with his son to improve his skills in that sport, but the elder Montana was also generous with his time in helping other kids. One of the most important achievements undertaken by Joe, Sr., in this regard was to start the first organized basketball program in

Theresa Montana gave her son, Joe, a kiss after he led the 49ers to victory over the Cincinnati Bengals in Super Bowl XVI on January 24, 1982. The man at right is not identified. Both of Montana's parents supported him in his sports endeavors as he was growing up. His father practiced with him nearly every day and started the first organized basketball program in Monongahela, Pennsylvania.

Monongahela. He rented a gym a few nights a week so that the boys could practice, and each kid paid a dollar to hire a janitor to clean up after them.

THE BLUE CHEVY CAPRICE

Joe, Sr., was also the driving force behind the creation of a regional league. By the time Joe was in junior high, the Monongahela team—with Joe Montana as its star point guard—was playing in regional tournaments all over the Northeast states. "Those were the most fun," Montana remembered, in a *Sports Illustrated* article. "The trips. We'd go anywhere. One night we played in a tournament in Bethel Park, Pennsylvania, then drove up to Niagara Falls [a distance of about 250 miles, or 400 kilo-meters] for another one, then back to Bethel Park for the finals."

Playing a variety of teams in this league gave the boys from Mon City valuable and varied experience. In a *Sporting News* article, teammate Brian Phillips recalled:

> I remember [Joe because of] a blue Chevy Caprice. That's the car his dad drove us around in, about eight or nine of us kids. He drove us all over the Pittsburgh area to play basketball. . . . Back then, it was obvious his dad was a big reason for Joe's success. His dad would get involved in everything Joe did, go to the practices, the games, all that stuff. His dad sometimes acted like everybody's dad.
>
> Another reason for Joe's success was those drives in that Caprice. Because we would go into other neighborhoods, sometimes tough, inner-city neighborhoods and play kids in basketball. And we would win. Just storm them. That made us tough.

AT RINGGOLD HIGH SCHOOL

Soon after Joe started his freshman year at Ringgold High School, he became interested in getting a part-time job. Some of his older cousins already worked to earn a little extra money, and he wanted to do the same. His parents, though, were concerned about Joe keeping up with his athletic activities and academic work.

So they made him a deal. They told him that, as long as he remained active in sports and maintained good grades, he did not have to get a job. They promised that they would make sure he always had what he needed.

Of course, what he *needed* was not always what he *wanted*. But it was good enough, and Joe accepted the deal. He kept his part of the bargain, too. He maintained a B average throughout high school and was even elected class vice president during his senior year.

Ringgold High had been created by combining two older schools. One of these had been in Monongahela, and the other in the nearby town of Donora. Both of these schools had very strong athletic traditions, and a number of future stars had attended them. For example, Stan Musial, the great slugger for the St. Louis Cardinals, and two more baseball greats, the father-son team of Ken Griffey, Sr., and Ken Griffey, Jr., all were born in Donora. (Junior was born in Donora but grew up in Cincinnati, where his father played. As a high school kid, Joe sometimes played baseball with Junior's uncle.)

Combining the schools of Donora and Monongahela had at first been the source of some concern. The Donora school was mostly African American, while the Monongahela school was mostly white. After the schools merged in the 1960s, there was indeed some occasional racial tension—but not when it came to sports, Joe said. He recalled, "The players on the teams got along fine—race was no big deal to us. We joked about it, that was all."

"I'M SERIOUS. HE COULD FLY."

At Ringgold, as might be expected, Joe stood out in every major sport. As a baseball player, he manned all the positions at one time or another and, as a batter, averaged just under .500. In basketball, he averaged 11 points a game as a junior and he led his team to a league championship as a senior. As with baseball, he played different positions on the basketball court: center, forward, and guard—sometimes all in the same game.

A lot of people who knew Joe then thought that he had even more potential and talent as a hoopster than as a football player—and he always said that basketball was his favorite sport. Fran LaMendola, Joe's basketball coach, said, "He could stand flat-footed and dunk with two hands." Teammate Brian Phillips added, "Joe was a great basketball player. Better than football, if you ask me. I've seen him play one-on-one, spot some guy eight points, and beat him, 10-8. Beat him with his left hand. Unbelievable leaping ability. I'm serious. He could fly."

Joe excelled even when he was merely filling in for other athletes in sports he did not usually play. He won the only tennis match he played. He made an informal 6-foot, 9-inch high jump. And he set a record during his only attempt at the discus.

Amazingly, though, he had a slow beginning on the high school football team. He joined the Ringgold Rams as a skinny, 6-foot, 165-pound (183-centimeter, 75-kilogram) sophomore. He stayed on the bench all that year, however, and even at the beginning of his junior year, it looked as if he might not be playing much.

CONFLICTS

This was because Joe was often in conflict with Ringgold's football coach, Chuck Abramski. One reason for this clash of personalities was that Joe chose to play American Legion baseball and summer basketball, both of them outside of school. This created a scheduling conflict. Joe could not take part in Abramski's rigorous weight-training program, which began well before the start of the football season.

Abramski was proud of his weight program, which he considered essential. According to Abramski, only Joe and one other player did not participate. (Memories differ on this: Assistant coach Jeff Petrucci says the figure was more like 20 percent to 30 percent of the squad, and some former players say the percentage of athletes who did not participate was even higher.)

In any case, Abramski was furious that a talented kid like Joe, someone who had the potential to be a star quarterback, was absent from the program. As a result, the coach withheld the privilege of playing time from him.

"JOE BANANA"

Another reason for Abramski's aversion to playing Joe was that Joe had earned a reputation for not being eager to turn out for practices. He disliked practices, mainly because he always had much more fun in games. For Joe, practicing basketball was a joy; he said, "I could practice basketball all day." Football practice, however, was simply hard work—a task to be endured so that he could actually play.

In particular, Joe recalls, he hated it when Coach Abramski made the team do wind sprints. This aversion to the exercise did not endear him to the coach. Abramski further ridiculed the teen by nicknaming him "Joe Banana."

Joe had a better relationship with Petrucci, the assistant coach who handled the quarterbacks. Joe felt that Petrucci had a good understanding of what caused a play to go wrong on the field and of what could be done quickly to fix such problems. As an adult, Montana has credited Petrucci with helping him develop his own foundation of skills in this regard, skills that let him swiftly and accurately analyze events on the field.

The relationship between the head coach and Joe, however, was not a total loss. Joe has admitted in later years that Abramski also taught him a lot, including valuable advice on how to throw on the run and how to scramble free from defenders. In *Sports Illustrated*, he said, "Chuck was a great coach in a lot of ways. He always tried to get the kids good equipment; he was always helping them get into college. I even wrote a letter of recommendation for him to go to another school after he left Ringgold. He was a fired-up, gung-ho coach, but he never got over the fact that I didn't take part in his summer weight program before my junior year. The man's all football."

BECOMING A STARTING QB

As a result of these conflicts, Joe's role on the football team was minimal during the early part of his junior year. Although Coach Abramski had considered using Joe as the starting quarterback, he decided against it. Abramski said that he was just doing what he felt was best. He commented, "It's very painful now, when people say I harbored this hatred for Joe. Hell, I loved the kid. I was doing what I thought was right for my squad."

Instead, he chose a player named Paul Timko, who was big but was not an accurate passer. With him at the helm, the team lost its season opener in a humiliating blowout. Ringgold won the next two games, but these were both forfeits caused by a teachers strike. Ringgold lost the two practice games that were played to fill in for the forfeits.

It became obvious that Timko was not going to work out as Abramski had planned. As a test, the coach had Joe take over

FIRING OFF AN APPLE CORE

In an article in *Sporting News*, one of Joe's teammates on the Ringgold High Rams, Joe Debranski, recalled this incidence of a Montana throw that was a spontaneous, mischievous prank:

We're lying on mats in a school hallway outside the high school cafeteria, resting during three-a-day practices one summer. All of us are eating fruit. You know. Dates, apples, pears. Well, our big tackle, Tank Tabarella, threw an apple core at Joe. He played dead for a second, then rose up and fired an apple core back at Tank.

Well, Tank ducked and the core flew into the cafeteria and hit one of the workers. Hit her good. Gave her a hurting. But Joe fell back down so fast, she never knew where it came from. People talk about that bullet he threw to Dwight Clark in that championship game as being his best pass ever. I know better.

as quarterback for some practice sessions. Joe had his work cut out for him during these practices, especially since Timko, who had been moved to defense, did his best to disrupt the new quarterback's moves and make him look bad. "Every day he just beat the hell out of me," Montana recalled in *Sports Illustrated*. "I'd be dead when I came home. Football wasn't much fun at that point."

But Joe stuck it out and performed well, and the coach opted to use him as a starter in the next regular game. He put Timko in at **tight end**—meaning that he and Joe needed to work closely together, not at cross-purposes. Joe recalled making sure that Timko got the ball a couple of times and stayed happy.

Coach Abramski may have regretted not using Joe sooner than he did. As that season and the next progressed, Joe played a major role in turning the Ringgold Rams around. With him at quarterback, the Rams made a dramatic turnaround and became a winning team.

AT THE HELM

This change was apparent from the beginning, as Montana had his first start against one of Ringgold's great rivals, Monessen High. Monessen had an intimidating lineup; Ringgold's **fullback**, Keith Bassi, recalled, "You had to be there. I mean Monessen had some players—Bubba Holmes, who went to Minnesota; Tony Benjamin, who went to Duke. The rumor was that guys there had been held back a year in nursery school so they'd be more mature when they hit high school."

As a result, no one thought the Ringgold Rams had much of a chance. After all, their record the year before, when Joe had still been on the bench, was 0–9. The outcome of the game with Monessen was especially in doubt because the Rams were facing a hostile away crowd.

With Joe leading the team, however, the Rams played hard and well. At halftime Ringgold led 21-7, and the final score was 34-34. The game ended in a tie, but it felt like a victory to the underdog Rams. Joe completed 12 passes in 22 attempts, for 223 yards and four touchdowns. Three of the touchdowns went to Timko, the tight end.

Zimmerman, the *Sports Illustrated* writer, described watching a videotape of Joe's first game as a high school starter, against Monessen, and seeing the confident moves that the quarterback would repeat as a pro:

> The first pass Montana threw against Monessen was on a scramble to his right; he pulled up and hit [Mike] Brantley, crossing underneath. The second was a sideline completion to Timko, neatly plunked between two defenders. The show was on. "They played a three-deep, where they give you the short stuff," said Frank Lawrence, who had been the offensive line coach. "Joe just killed 'em with timed patterns." It was an eerie feeling, watching Montana drop back from **center**, set, and throw. All his 49er mechanics were there, the quick setup, the nifty glide to the outside, scrambling but under control, buying time, looking for a receiver underneath. It seemed as if he had been doing it all his life, and this was a kid in his first high school start. "Watch Joe now," Lawrence said as Ringgold scored on a one-yard plunge. "See that? He backpedals after the touchdown and throws his hands up. Same mannerisms as now."

That year continued to see major improvement. With Joe as the team's starting quarterback, Ringgold posted a 4–3–2 record. During Joe's senior year, the difference was even more dramatic; the Rams' record improved to 8–1. The team lost in the playoffs during a game played in the sleet with three starters injured.

Joe's performance was so strong during his senior year that he was named to *Parade* magazine's All-American team. A number of college football scouts were paying careful attention

Joe Montana celebrated after teammate Dexter Carter scored a 74-yard touchdown in December 1990 against the Los Angeles Rams. Montana struck this image often over the years. Beginning way back in high school, Montana would celebrate a touchdown by throwing his arms in the air.

to him by this time. These scouts were fully aware of the heritage and reputation of the Monongahela Valley; all of them were on the lookout for the next Namath or Unitas.

ON TO SOUTH BEND, INDIANA

Joe, however, was still considered as powerful a basketball player as anything else, and the college basketball scouts were also checking him out. In fact, it was an open question right until the end of his high school years: Would Joe choose hoops or the gridiron for his college career?

Several schools and programs wooed him. One was North Carolina State University, which offered Joe a basketball scholarship that he thought seriously about accepting.

THE SCOUTS COME TO RINGGOLD HIGH

When Joe Montana was a senior in high school, college scouts were quite aware of his talent and were busily trying to make friends with his father, Joe, Sr. Bob Osleger, who was then the golf coach at Ringgold High School, recalled, in a *Sports Illustrated* article, what football games were like at the school in those days:

In his senior year, the games at Legion Field were a happening. There was this flat bit of ground above the stadium, and Joe's father would stand there and watch the game, and all these college coaches and scouts would vie for position to stand near him. The whispers would start, about which college coaches were there that night, and I can see it so clearly now. Joe's dad would be standing there with his hands in his pockets and all these guys jockeying for position around him.

But Joe also made trips to check out several other schools. Plus, he was not firmly committed to basketball. He finally decided to focus on football, feeling that his greatest strength was in that sport.

He decided to accept an offer from the University of Notre Dame in South Bend, Indiana. Joe had been a fan of Notre Dame's legendary football team, the Fighting Irish, ever since he had been a little kid. He recalled, "I don't even remember how I got started on Notre Dame. I really liked the team. It was almost like a religion; I couldn't do anything until I watched the game on Saturday or Sunday if they were on [television]."

So Joe was naturally enthusiastic about joining the Irish and was delighted when Notre Dame offered him a slot. Following his graduation from high school in 1974, he headed for Indiana. Joe's college years were about to begin.

Joe College

The University of Notre Dame has a long and distinguished tradition of excellence in football. The school's early history includes a winning streak of 27 games that began in 1910. Since that remarkable feat, the Notre Dame football program has racked up 11 NCAA football championships, more than 800 all-time wins, and a 73.9 percent winning record—the best in college football.

Many famous names are connected with the Fighting Irish. (The nickname probably comes from Irish immigrants who fought during the American Civil War.) Among the more illustrious are Notre Dame's seven Heisman Trophy winners, including Paul Hornung in 1956, John Lujack in 1947, and Angelo Bertelli in 1943.

The school's coaches, meanwhile, have included the likes of Knute Rockne, considered by many to be the greatest college football coach in the history of the sport. Notre Dame has also been home to such legends as The Four Horsemen (who formed the backbone of the Fighting Irish's mighty 1924 team) and George Gipp, "the Gipper," whose untimely death was immortalized by Ronald Reagan's portrayal of him in the 1940 film *Knute Rockne, All American*.

Not surprisingly, Joe Montana was fully aware of all of this history when he arrived in South Bend, Indiana, as an 18-year-old freshman in the fall of 1974. He knew that he was about to become part of a longstanding tradition of stellar football. Montana says now that the prospect of attending the college completely awed him. He commented, "I tell you I was intimidated by Notre Dame from the day I stepped on campus. In a lot of ways there's a lot more pressure there than there is in the NFL."

HOMESICK

The transition Montana had to make from life in Mon City to college life in South Bend was rough at first. During his freshman year, he was frequently homesick—understandably so, since he was living a long way from the only place that had ever been home to him.

To help his homesickness, Montana called his parents several times a week. He especially wanted to talk with Joe, Sr., who was still the teen's closest friend. One of Montana's teammates at Notre Dame, Steve Orsini, confirmed this, commenting in *Sports Illustrated* that "the person Joe felt closest to was back in Monongahela."

For his part, Joe, Sr., came to visit Notre Dame whenever he could. He would occasionally drive the eight hours to South Bend to watch his son in an afternoon scrimmage. They would grab a bite to eat, hang out for a while, and then Joe, Sr., would drive home to be at work the next day. Montana's freshman

The mural known as "Touchdown Jesus" overlooks the stadium at the University of Notre Dame in South Bend, Indiana. The tradition of football excellence is a strong one at Notre Dame, whose teams have won 11 national titles and more than 800 games.

roommate, Nick DeCicco, recalled, "His dad would sometimes show up in the middle of the night, and we'd all go out at 1 A.M. for a stack of pancakes. It was crazy."

Even with this support, it was still a tough transition for the freshman. Back in Mon City, Montana had been a star athlete in a small town that treasured its athletes—in other words, he had been a big fish in a small pond. At Notre Dame, however, he felt lost in the shuffle. He was just one of many promising student-athletes. Furthermore, Montana struggled during that first year with his studies. Notre Dame's academic standards were (and still are) notoriously rigorous.

FRIENDS AND A BRIEF MARRIAGE

Still, Montana tried to keep his feelings of homesickness hidden from most of the people he knew. He persevered as best he could, and gradually his outlook improved. He began to feel more comfortable, his grades got better, and he made a few good and lasting friends.

One of these was his roommate, Nick DeCicco. DeCicco's father was the school's fencing coach and also the football team's academic adviser. Montana's best friend at school, meanwhile, was Mark Ewald, who was, like Montana, at Notre Dame to play both basketball and football.

Montana's feelings of loneliness lessened even more when he married his high school sweetheart, Kim Moses, partway through his freshman year. After the wedding, Kim moved to South Bend from Monongahela and found work in Notre Dame's sports-information office. After the games, Joe would keep Kim company as she typed up the team's statistics in the sports office.

It was good for Montana to have a familiar face from his hometown around. The marriage, however, did not last, and the couple divorced after three years. About the failure of this early marriage, Montana said simply, "We were too young."

FRESHMAN YEAR ON THE BENCH

Montana had been one of Ringgold High's star players, but at an elite program like Notre Dame he was just one of many outstanding athletes. In fact, of the players who were on the Notre Dame football team during the years Montana was there, 46 were drafted by the NFL, eight of them in the first round. So Montana was nearly lost on the Fighting Irish's very deep bench.

In fact, he was just one of seven quarterbacks on the roster during his freshman year. Among them were Gary Forystek, who, like Montana, had been a *Parade* magazine All-American in high school; Rick Slager, a force at Notre Dame in both football and tennis; and Tom Clements, who was also a Pennsylvania boy. More to the point, Clements had been the starter on the Irish's national championship team the previous year.

As a result of this abundance of talent, Montana did not play on the varsity team during his freshman year. He did play on the junior varsity squad but only in three games. He completed a grand total of one pass that year.

Instead, Montana spent the majority of his freshman year on the scout team. This meant that, in practices, Montana had to pretend to be the quarterback of the team the Irish were going to face next. As a result, Montana spent most of that first year being mercilessly pounded by Notre Dame's punishing first-string defense—or, as he put it, "They took turns beating up on me."

COMING INTO HIS OWN

The school's football coach that year, Ara Parseghian, was a living legend—Notre Dame's most successful football coach in modern times. Montana, though, spent only one season under him. After 11 years with the Fighting Irish, Parseghian decided he was ready for rest and retirement.

He was wrapping up an outstanding career. During the so-called Era of Ara, Notre Dame had been among the top 15 teams in the country every year. Montana later remarked that he was sorry to see Parseghian go. The coach was not only a great leader, Montana felt, but he was also easygoing and likable.

Coach Parseghian's replacement, beginning in 1975, was Dan Devine, who had had a distinguished coaching career with Arizona State University, the University of Missouri, and the Green Bay Packers. Devine thought that Montana was a promising player, commenting later, "He just impressed me as the kind of guy who you think is going to get the job done."

Still, Devine did not play Montana very much at first during Montana's sophomore year. In fact, Montana stayed on the bench for the first two games of the season because Rick Slager was Devine's favored quarterback. Ken MacAfee, an All-America tight end at Notre Dame who went on to play for the 49ers, still wonders why. In an article in *Time*, MacAfee said, "The pattern began to be that Rick Slager would start the game, and then Montana would have to come in and save it."

"WHO'S JOE MONTANA?"

Notre Dame's legendary football coach, Ara Parseghian, resigned for health and personal reasons late in 1974, and the coach for the next season was Dan Devine, who was coming from a stint with the Green Bay Packers. In *Sports Illustrated*, Devine recalled:

I asked the coaches about my quarterbacks when I first got there. No one said much about Joe. He'd been something like the seventh or eighth quarterback. Then he had a fine spring practice, really outstanding. I came home and told my wife, "I'm gonna start Joe Montana in the final spring game," and she said, "Who's Joe Montana?" I said, "He's the guy who's going to feed our family for the next few years."

In the third game of the season, against Northwestern, Notre Dame was trailing 7-0 when Slager got hurt. Devine sent Montana in, and Montana proceeded to demonstrate his skills—in particular his talent for inspiring a team to come from behind. At the game's end, the Irish had trampled Northwestern, 31-7.

THE COMEBACK KID COMES THROUGH

After that performance, Montana played more often. He was still not the starter, a source of understandable aggravation to him and a mystery to the other players. Whatever the case, he helped lead the Irish to several more victories, including notable wins over North Carolina and Air Force.

In the North Carolina game, Notre Dame was down 14-6 in the fourth quarter. Then The Comeback Kid—as Montana was starting to be called—provided the spark that Notre Dame needed. With just over six minutes left, Montana threw two touchdowns, one of them an 80-yard game winner, for a final score of 21-14.

The Air Force game provided a similar chain of events. With Notre Dame trailing 30-10 in the fourth quarter, Montana entered the game with 13 minutes to go and led the team to three quick touchdowns, running for one and passing for another. The game ended with a squeaker of a victory for Notre Dame, 31-30.

Unfortunately, Montana ran into some bad luck later that season. He broke his finger and was forced to sit out the rest of the year. Another injury plagued him the following season, his junior year: Montana separated his throwing shoulder and was forced to sit out the entire season.

A REDSHIRT AND A NATIONAL VICTORY

The injury was a bad one—so bad that Montana wondered if his football career might be over. His shoulder, however, healed well. By the start of the next season, Montana was ready to

After Joe Montana's first year at Notre Dame, Dan Devine became the coach of the Fighting Irish. Devine did not use Montana as a starting quarterback right away, and several of Montana's teammates wondered why.

rejoin the active list as a **redshirt** junior. (Redshirt refers to a college player who skips a year of play without losing a year of eligibility. College athletes are only eligible to play four years.)

Montana, however, still had to face his ongoing conflict with Coach Devine, who refused to let him begin the season as the starting quarterback. Montana, instead, was the No. 3 quarterback.

Devine later claimed that Montana had not been medically cleared to play at that point, but this was news to everyone, most of all Montana, and no one could understand why Devine was not playing him. Ken MacAfee said in *Sports Illustrated*, "When we lost to Mississippi [20-13 in the second game of the season] with Joe on the bench, I thought, 'What a weird deal.' I mean we all knew he could do it, he knew he could do it, but he wasn't playing. He was really down. I remember going to his apartment one night and he said, 'I'm just sick of this crap, sick of the whole thing.'"

Then, in the third game of the season, with Notre Dame losing 24-14 to Purdue, Devine brought The Comeback Kid off the bench. Montana did not disappoint: He threw for 154 yards and a touchdown in the final 11 minutes, giving the Irish a 31-24 victory.

After that performance, Devine finally relented and made Montana his starting quarterback. His decision turned out to be a good one. Notre Dame did not lose again that season, and won a place in the 1978 Cotton Bowl. There, the Fighting Irish were matched against the top-ranked, heavily favored University of Texas Longhorns. But the Fighting Irish dominated the game, never trailing, and beat the Longhorns 38-10 to take the national championship.

JUGGLING ACADEMICS AND ATHLETICS

All through his college years, Montana worked hard to improve his football moves, those traits that set him apart as a player. For example, he refined his already excellent instinct for knowing when a receiver would get open. He also perfected the accuracy of his throwing arm.

And he boosted both his degree of calm under pressure and his self-confidence about winning against tough odds—attributes crucial to inspiring the rest of the team.

Joe Montana heaves a pass downfield during a game against the University of Southern California at Notre Dame Stadium. Montana had to sit out a year with a shoulder injury, and he finally became Notre Dame's starting quarterback during his junior year.

NFL **noseguard** Bob Golic, who played at Notre Dame with Montana, recalled, "Whenever he came on the field, the players knew they had a friend coming in." NFL **free safety** Dave Waymer, who started his Notre Dame career as a wideout, adds, "When the pressure came, we knew he was the guy who wouldn't overheat."

Academically, Montana was also holding his own. He majored in business and did reasonably well, earning mostly Bs and Cs. He struggled at times, however; during his sophomore year he was on academic probation, and at one point he failed accounting—a crucial class for a business major. Luckily, that class was the only one he ever flunked.

During most summers, when school was out, Montana stayed in South Bend. For Montana, the main advantage to this was that he could take extra courses, which made juggling schoolwork and athletics easier during the regular school year. In addition to summer school, Montana also worked at a variety of part-time jobs. One year he cooked in a restaurant. During another he worked for the city's parks department, dragging baseball fields and liming baselines. And one summer he found a job doing market research.

Through it all, Joe remained a—well, a regular Joe. Dave Huffman, who was Montana's center at Notre Dame and went on to be a guard with the Minnesota Vikings, remembered him as "just a regular guy who wanted to play hoops, go drink a beer. We called him Joe Montanalow because he was the spitting image of [singer] Barry Manilow. In his senior year he moved into an apartment above a bar. When the bar closed down, we'd go upstairs to Joe's place. It was our after-hours joint."

During the school year, Montana had not only his commitment to football and his academic responsibilities; he was also playing basketball for Digger Phelps, the legendary Notre Dame hoops coach. Although his football prospects clearly improved every year, Montana had not given up entirely on basketball. He hit his stride in that sport in the spring of his senior year, as a member of the team that won the Bookstore Tournament, a prestigious monthlong competition featuring squads made up of Notre Dame students, faculty, and staff.

THE '79 COTTON BOWL

During Montana's senior year, the Notre Dame football team had another outstanding season. The final regular-season game, against the University of Southern California, was the one that Montana considered the best of his college career. In that contest, the Irish were trailing badly in the fourth quarter,

24-6, but Montana was able to bring them back to take the lead, 25-24. At the last moment, USC kicked a **field goal** to clinch the victory, 27-25.

Notre Dame lost, but for Montana it was still a terrific game. In the second half, he completed more passes, 17, than he ever had in a full game before that. Afterward, Montana received an honorable mention in the All-American voting for the second year in a row.

Furthermore, Notre Dame had such an outstanding season that it again won the right to compete in the Cotton Bowl. In that contest, Montana capped his college career with a victory that, to many of his fans, remains the most memorable of all his college games. This was an amazing match at the Cotton Bowl against the University of Houston Cougars.

January 1, 1979, was a freakishly cold day in Dallas, just 20° above zero (-7°Celsius), with winds of 30 miles per hour (48 kilometers per hour), in a town normally known for its temperate winters. People in the stadium had to knock ice off their seats before they could sit, and an inch of ice coated the stadium's artificial turf. As if the inclement weather was not bad enough, Montana was suffering from the flu and felt terrible. But he was determined to play in this, his final college game.

By halftime, Montana was in rough condition. He was shaking uncontrollably from the cold, and his body temperature had dropped to 96° (35.5°Celsius). He said, "I felt like I was sitting in a bucket of ice." The team was in bad shape, too; at one point it had led 12-0 but was now trailing 20-12.

Montana was forced to retire to the locker room. Notre Dame's coaches and training staff fed him chicken bouillon and wrapped him in blankets, successfully bringing his body temperature back to normal. He sat out most of the third quarter as his team fell further behind, 34-12. Then, in the fourth quarter, Montana was considered fit to return.

He went back into the game and took over right away, quickly chipping into his team's deficit. After Notre Dame scored on a blocked punt, Montana passed for a **two-point conversion**. When Notre Dame regained possession of the ball, he ran for a touchdown and passed for another two points. Now the Irish were only six points behind. But, with less than two minutes remaining, Montana **fumbled** and Houston recovered the ball.

"NOT EXACTLY A MIGHTY ROAR"

The crowning moment of Joe Montana's college career was his stunning comeback victory in frigid weather at the 1979 Cotton Bowl in Dallas. During the third quarter, suffering from hypothermia, Montana was forced to sit in the locker room while his team fell behind.

In a *Sports Illustrated* article, coach Dan Devine recalled, "Rick Slager was in law school then, and he was a graduate assistant coach on the sidelines with me. His job was to run into the locker room every five minutes to see what Joe's temperature was. He'd come back and say, 'It's up to 97°,' and five minutes later I'd tell him to run in and find out again."

With 7:37 left in the fourth quarter, Montana was pronounced well enough to rejoin the game. When he came running onto the field, a mighty roar came from the crowd.

"Uh, no, not exactly a mighty roar," said Dave Huffman, the Notre Dame center, in the *Sports Illustrated* article. "More like a feeble, frozen roar, since there were only a few people left in the stands, and ice was falling out of their mouths. Actually, I didn't even know Joe was out there until I felt his hands taking the snap. I thought, Wait a minute, these are different hands."

THIRTY SECONDS LEFT AND A STUNNING VICTORY

On fourth-and-one in its own territory, with 30 seconds remaining, Houston decided to go for a **first down**—a questionable decision—but the Cougars came up short. Notre Dame got the ball again on the 29-yard line and moved it down to the 8-yard line. Six seconds left.

Devine called a pass to Kris Haines in the corner of the end zone, but Montana threw the ball too low and Haines slipped and could not get it. Two seconds left. Montana asked Haines if he thought he could get it again, and Haines said yes. So, when Devine asked Montana what he recommended for the last play, Montana said the Irish should try the same one as before.

In an article in *Time*, Haines remembered: "We went back into the huddle with two seconds to go, and Joe said, 'Don't worry, you can do it.' He gave me that little half-smile of his and called the exact same play again, right on the money for the touchdown." Devine added, from a *Sports Illustrated* article, "With the noseguard staring him in the face, Joe threw a perfect pass, low and outside, a bullet—under all that pressure, with terrible conditions. He was so calm. I swear to God he was no different than he would have been in practice."

That stunning play tied the game at 34-34. Notre Dame got the extra point but was penalized for illegal motion. Joe Unis, the placekicker, tried again, and the kick was good. The Irish had won, 35-34, and Joe Montana's college football career ended with an astonishing victory—23 points scored in just seven-and-a-half minutes, erasing Houston's seemingly overwhelming lead of 22 points.

Montana was exhausted beyond words when it was over. The Notre Dame trainers and doctors spent a long time with him, making sure he was fine. By the time Montana got back to the hotel, all of his teammates were gone. So Montana sat in the hallway of their hotel with a case of beer and celebrated the victory by himself.

Joe Montana slipped out of the arms of University of Houston defender Fred Snell during the final drive of the 1979 Cotton Bowl. Montana was suffering from the flu and did not play for much of the second half. He returned in the fourth quarter and led the Fighting Irish as they scored 23 unanswered points to beat Houston 35-34.

"I WANTED TO THAW OUT"

After crowning his collegiate football career with that feat, Montana graduated. He had a degree in business and marketing. More exciting, he had a strong chance of being drafted by the pros. (As in high school, Montana had been torn between concentrating on football or basketball after graduating. In the end, football prevailed.)

First, however, came a move away from Indiana. Montana was tired of the fierce Midwest winters, and he did not stay in South Bend any longer than necessary. He moved instead to Manhattan Beach, near Los Angeles in Southern California. He lived there with one of his cousins, in an apartment above a bar coincidentally called Joe's. "I'd had enough winters," Montana commented. "I wanted to thaw out."

Of course, the pro scouts were aware that he had moved. They had their eyes on him, although not all of them were completely enthusiastic. Many reported on what they felt was only average arm strength and other faults.

Scouts typically rated Montana a 6 or 6½ out of a possible 9 in their reports. One commented that Montana could thread the needle—that is, complete a difficult pass through a narrow opening between several defenders at different depths. However, the scout wrote, according to *Sports Illustrated*, "He usually goes with his primary receiver and forces the ball to him even when he's in a crowd. He's a gutty, gambling, cocky type. Doesn't have great tools but could eventually start."

Despite such less-than-glowing reports, there were strong nibbles from the pros. Montana worked out with the Los Angeles Rams near his new Southern California home. The New York Giants flew him east for a tryout.

And, about two weeks before the **draft**, he worked out for Sam Wyche, who was then the quarterbacks coach for the San Francisco 49ers. Montana recalled, "He was putting me through different footwork drills and watching me throw different passes. . . . I did a lot of things he liked. I didn't throw the ball as hard as I could every play. I just made the different passes he wanted me to throw."

THE DRAFT

On the day of the 1979 draft, Montana and his agent, Larry Muno, went to a restaurant in Manhattan Beach called The Kettle to await the results. The draft was not as hugely popular an event as it is now, and it was not televised. To learn about new developments, Muno called his office every 10 minutes or so.

The first two rounds went by, and Montana's name was not called. He began to worry. In an interview with the *Contra*

Costa Times, he recalled, "People said I would be picked in the first or second round. When I was getting passed, I was getting anxious."

Then came the word: The 49ers took Montana as the last pick in the third round. (There has been much speculation over the years as to why he was picked so late. No one seems to have an adequate explanation.)

Montana was the eighty-second overall pick in that year's draft. He was the fourth quarterback chosen, behind Jack Thompson (who went to the Cincinnati Bengals), Phil Simms (to the New York Giants), and Steve Fuller (to the Kansas City Chiefs). Montana was not even the 49ers' first pick that year; wide receiver James Owens from UCLA had that honor.

But the 49ers' new coach, Bill Walsh, said that he was pleased with the way it turned out. "It really didn't take long to decide on Joe," he recalled. "His quickness, the only person I could connect with that was Joe Namath, who had the quickest feet of any quarterback I had ever seen. Joe Montana had the same quickness, agility and fluid movement that Namath had. And he threw the ball fine in our drills."

ON TO SAN FRANCISCO

For his part, Montana was disappointed not to have been chosen in the first round, since those players usually could command more money when it came time to negotiate contracts. Nonetheless, he was happy to be headed to the 49ers. "I was excited," he recalled. "It was a great opportunity coming to a great city. . . . I was just excited to get that opportunity with them."

And, as every sports fan knows, it turned out to be a match made in heaven, one that would turn the 49ers' fortunes around and make Joe Montana a superstar. Writer Cam Inman commented that the decision by the 49ers to take Montana was "a choice that altered the course of their franchise unlike any other draft pick in their history." That change in direction was about to start.

The Early 49ers Years

When the San Francisco 49ers signed Joe Montana in 1979, the team was in terrible shape. It had struggled for most of the '70s; the low point came in 1978, when the team had a bitterly disappointing 2–14 record for the season. This dismal figure reflected the 49ers' dubious distinction of being the lowest-scoring organization in pro football that year. They only scored 219 points that season, or an average of 13.7 points per game.

The 49ers' reputation was so poor that a number of Montana's friends were shocked that he could be enthusiastic about heading to the team. Why would such a talented player be excited about joining the worst pro team in the country? Montana predicted, however, with characteristic confidence, that the 49ers would not *always* be the worst.

He was right.

IN TRAINING CAMP

Montana's three-year contract with the 49ers paid him a $50,000 signing bonus and an escalating base salary of $50,000, $70,000, and $85,000 for the three years. These are paltry sums by today's multimillion-dollar standards for pro athletes, and even for the period they were hardly top dollar. (As a comparison, another star quarterback, Joe Namath, signed as a rookie with the Jets in 1965 for a then-record $400,000.) Still, it was good money—good enough for Montana, at least, when he reported to training camp that year.

At the camp, many observers noticed how small and thin the new recruit seemed to be. And, by some standards, he was; in fact, the 49ers apparently felt it necessary to fudge the figures a

JUST A SLAPPY

One of the main attributes that everybody who knows Joe Montana comments on is the amazing sense of calm, low-key self-confidence he carries with him. Brian Billick was the assistant director of public relations for the 49ers when Montana was drafted by the team. It was Billick's job to pick up the rookie when he arrived in San Francisco at the airport. In an article by Cam Inman, Billick recalled:

Nobody knew what we were getting. He was a slappy out of Notre Dame that showed potential and signs. Bill [Walsh] saw more in Joe than a lot of people did. When I went to pick him up [at the airport], I was picking up some slappy, third-round draft choice. There was a quality about Joe, even then. There was a calmness in Joe's eyes you didn't typically see as a rookie.

bit. The team's official media guide for that year listed Montana as 6 feet 3 inches and 200 pounds (190.5 centimeters and 91 kilograms). Actually, he stood 6-foot-2 (188 centimeters) and weighed barely 185 pounds (84 kilograms).

Montana's roommate during that rookie training camp became a good friend. He was another rookie, wide receiver Dwight Clark. Clark had played college ball at Clemson University in South Carolina.

In those early days, Clark was unsure of himself; he was not certain that he had enough talent to stay in the NFL. Clark confided to Montana that he was scared every morning of camp, afraid that he would hear John McVay, who was the director of player personnel, say the dreaded words: "Bill wants to see you." To Clark, this was a sure sign that the team's new coach, Bill Walsh, was about to make a cut.

Montana says now that he was pretty sure that he would not be cut. Only one other quarterback on the 49ers, Steve DeBerg, had much experience, and DeBerg was still recovering from knee surgery. So Montana figured that his own chances of survival were pretty good. Nonetheless, Montana says, to make his friend feel better he acted as if he were also worried. Fortunately for football history, neither of them heard McVay speak those frightening words.

"AS SMART AS THEY COME IN FOOTBALL"

Walsh, the new coach, had joined the 49ers just months before the draft that brought in Montana. Walsh had most recently come from a head-coaching position at Stanford University. Before that, he had been an assistant coach with the Oakland Raiders, the Cincinnati Bengals, and the San Diego Chargers.

From the beginning, Montana had high regard for the coach's abilities. He once remarked, "Walsh is as smart as they come in football." For his part, Walsh could see the skinny quarterback's potential. Although many people considered Montana a questionable choice—he was relatively

San Francisco 49ers coach Bill Walsh and Joe Montana conferred on the sidelines during a game in 1981. Montana's abilities as a quarterback fit in well with the innovative, pass-dependent offense that Walsh wanted to run.

small and slow, and his arm strength was not as powerful as it could have been—Walsh believed that Montana had something special.

That something special fit in well with the innovative system that Walsh was developing. This system emphasized passing over running. Walsh's strategy, which eventually became known as the "**West Coast offense**," needed someone like Montana. At its heart was a quarterback who could rely more on agility and accuracy than on sheer power—someone who could throw with precision and adjust quickly to the opposing team's defensive strategy.

Any quarterback Walsh used also needed to be quick-witted. A typical NFL team might go into a game with 15 running plays and 30 passing plays. Walsh had his team learn at least 30 running plays and 80 to 90 passing plays. A tremendous amount of memorization was needed, especially since two formations were designed for most passing plays.

THE WORST JOB IN THE WORLD

Walsh and Montana not only respected each other's abilities; they also got along well personally. Nonetheless, the beginning of their relationship was tentative, a period of gradually getting to know each other. Walsh wanted to move slowly before putting Montana, now wearing No. 16, into a position of responsibility.

So the coach's first decision regarding Montana was to make him the holder for the placekicker. Montana describes this position as the worst job in the world. "Do it perfectly, nobody notices," he said. "Do it wrong, everybody notices." Because he filled this necessary but lowly role, Montana appeared in all 16 of the 49ers' games in 1979—although frequently he was just the holder.

He did not get a chance to throw his first NFL pass until the third game of the season, against the Los Angeles Rams. Not until two months later did Montana throw his first touchdown pass—his only one of the season—in a game against the Denver Broncos. His first start came two games after that, against the St. Louis Cardinals.

In short, Montana did not play much that first season. He threw a total of only 23 passes. Walsh clearly wanted to break his new quarterback in slowly. "As a rookie on a poor team," Walsh recalled in *Time* magazine, "he did a fair job, is all. But his skills were obvious. He was just so active, so quick on his feet, so instinctive. The second year, we eased him in carefully, so as not to break him." Elsewhere, the coach commented, "We didn't want to throw him to the wolves. We thought it was important to give him moments of success early, to build his confidence."

THE BEGINNINGS OF GREATNESS

At the start of the 1980 season, Walsh still felt that Montana was not ready to start regularly, or even play much. He kept the quarterback on the sidelines until the third game of the season, against the New York Jets. In that game, Montana showed a glimpse of what he could do; he ran for a touchdown and threw for another.

After that, DeBerg and Montana alternated as the team's quarterback. DeBerg, who had joined the 49ers in 1978, had compiled a decent record with San Francisco. It was Walsh's opinion, however, that Montana represented the team's best chances in the long run. In the short run, meanwhile, alternating the quarterbacks had two advantages. It gave Montana an increasing amount of experience. It also kept the team's opponents off guard, since they were never sure whom they would be facing.

During the 1980 season, Montana continued to make progress. He started seven of the season's last 10 games, including the last five in a row. These final five games marked the first of 49 straight starts for Montana—a streak that did not end until injury sidelined him in 1984. The 49ers, meanwhile, showed their faith in Montana by trading DeBerg to the Denver

Broncos after the 1980 season and making Montana their starting quarterback.

THE COMEBACK KID STRIKES AGAIN

One game at the end of 1980 was a memorable contest against the New Orleans Saints. Although New Orleans was having a terrible year—it was 0–13—it nonetheless had some hope of winning. After all, it was facing San Francisco, a 5–8 team whose reputation at that point was nearly as dismal.

The Saints managed to dominate the first half, and they were up 35-7 at halftime. In the fourth quarter, though, Montana rallied, leading his team in another of his patented comebacks. The 49ers caught up with the Saints to tie the score at 35-35 in the game's final minutes. Then Ray Wersching kicked a field goal in overtime, and the 49ers were victorious, 38-35.

The 49ers' comeback set a record for the most points ever overcome to win a regular-season NFL game. The game was also the first of the 26 fourth-quarter comebacks that Montana would eventually achieve with the 49ers.

The 49ers were making dramatic improvements. In 1979, Montana's rookie year, San Francisco had a 2–14 record (the same as the year before). In Montana's second year, the Niners had improved to 6–10. And in 1981, his third year, the team achieved the best record in the NFL: 13–3. A well-executed offense, along with an overhauled defense, sparked the team's turnaround. Montana himself had a spectacular year that third season, completing 311 of 488 passes (a 63.7 completion percentage) for 3,565 yards and 19 touchdowns.

"RESPECT THAT!"

In the 1981 divisional playoffs, the 49ers faced a formidable opponent, the New York Giants—and beat them 38-24. Next up was the NFC Championship Game, which pitted San Francisco against the Dallas Cowboys.

The Cowboys were also powerful opponents. Dallas was a perennial postseason powerhouse and had made it to five Super Bowls. The 49ers, on the other hand, had played for 36 seasons without winning a single conference or league title. San Francisco also had a history of losing games to the Cowboys.

Furthermore, San Francisco's running game was unimpressive, and its defense was talented but inconsistent. Dallas, meanwhile, boasted such outstanding players as running back Tony Dorsett and middle linebacker/defensive tackle Randy White (both of whom, incidentally, came from the same part of Pennsylvania as Montana).

In short, the Cowboys were heavily favored, and it was going to be an uphill battle for the 49ers.

In the days before the game, Dallas waged cutting psychological warfare. For example, Ed "Too Tall" Jones, a defensive end for the Cowboys, told reporters that he had no respect for the 49ers. During the game, a stung Montana got even for this insult.

On one play, a naked **bootleg**, he faked to the outside as "Too Tall" came after him. Jones took the fake, Montana pulled up, Jones fell down, and the quarterback threw a successful 38-yard pass to Dwight Clark. Montana then yelled, "Respect that!" to Jones. He had to do it at the top of his lungs, however, because the roar of the cheering crowd was so loud.

Throughout the game, the 49ers played well, but it was a close contest and the Cowboys managed to take and hold the lead until late in the fourth quarter—time for the unflappable Montana to go to work. The 49ers were down 27-21 and on their own 11-yard line, with 4:54 left in the game. As Montana dryly commented later, "Plenty of time to go 89 yards."

MOVING UP THE FIELD

The 49ers managed to get some good yardage and move the ball just across midfield into Cowboy territory, but by then, only two minutes were left in the game. The pressure was tremendous. Offensive lineman Randy Cross, who was fighting the flu, was so stressed out that he threw up in the huddle.

Wide receiver Freddie Solomon ran a double **reverse** for 14 yards—and then Montana got lucky. He threw a pass that he thought Cowboys cornerback Everson Walls would knock down (Walls had already intercepted Montana twice during the game). Instead, the cornerback just grazed it.

Clark caught the pass, putting the 49ers on the 25-yard line. Solomon caught still another pass, and San Francisco was on the 13-yard line with 1:15 left.

After a timeout, Walsh called a pass to Solomon. Solomon was open, but Montana missed him. Second down. Lenvil Elliott carried the ball to the 6-yard line. Now it was third and three. Another timeout, with 58 seconds left.

Walsh called a play that had Clark flanking out to the right, with Solomon in the slot to Montana's left. Clark was supposed to cut to his left with Solomon cutting under him to the right, to the corner. The idea was that Clark would pick off the defense and Solomon would be open in the corner. If Solomon was not open, Montana was to look for Clark.

"I HEARD THE TOUCHDOWN"

As this crucial play began, prospects did not look good for Montana. The Cowboys defended the play perfectly, and the quarterback had three opponents closing in on him, including Too Tall Jones. Montana was backpedaling toward the right sideline, and a **sack** seemed inevitable. Furthermore, Montana's primary receiver, Solomon, was covered.

So he went to Plan B and looked for Clark. Montana could not see Clark, but he knew where the wide receiver should have been. At the last moment, a stumbling, off-balance Montana threw off his back foot, sending the ball toward the back right corner of the end zone.

Afterward, many observers commented that they thought Montana was trying to throw the ball away to keep San Francisco

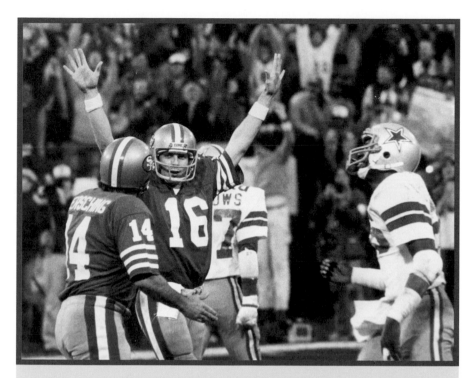

Joe Montana raised his arms in celebration after Ray Wersching *(left)* kicked an extra point to give the 49ers a 28-27 lead with less than a minute to go in the NFC Championship Game on January 10, 1982. With the victory, the 49ers were going to their first-ever Super Bowl.

in position to try again on the **fourth down**. But both players say that they had practiced this very play many times before. Montana has said that Walsh had made them practice it at the end of every 49ers workout.

In theory, therefore, Clark and Montana knew the play cold. But, as every athlete knows, the difference between theory and reality can be vast. There was no guarantee that it would be successful.

But it was. The ball went high and seemed to be sailing out of play. Then Clark, in the end zone, rose up into the air and caught the pass with the tips of his fingers, just getting his feet in for the touchdown.

Meanwhile, Montana got knocked down, so he never saw Clark's amazing leap—but he knew that it had worked. "I heard it," Montana recalled. "I heard the touchdown. I heard it from the San Francisco fans, who were screaming."

THE CATCH

This spectacular play tied the score at 27-27, and the successful extra point gave the 49ers a one-point lead with 51 seconds left. Dallas needed only a field goal to win, but the 49er defense was able to contain the Cowboys in the remaining seconds. Cowboys safety Charlie Waters commented in a *Time* magazine article, "We stopped them pretty good most of the game. But that last drive for some reason was unstoppable."

And so San Francisco carried the day. It had clinched the NFC championship. The 49ers were headed to the Super Bowl for the first time.

Back in the locker room, the ecstatic team screamed and yelled—and then collapsed. Montana found himself lying on the floor, overjoyed but so exhausted that he could not even get up until the team's equipment manager helped him.

That winning Montana-Clark play was destined to become one of the most famous in NFL history. It has become universally known as "The Catch." Some observers feel that this is a misnomer, because it implies that Clark was the hero of the day. They point out that there could have been no Catch without a Pass, and for that, Clark needed Montana's instincts and abilities.

Both players give the other credit. Clark said, "To me, it was just another episode of Montana magic. He put the ball exactly where he had to." For his part, Montana remarked, "The play has always been called The Catch, and that's just what it was: The Catch. It wasn't a bad pass—I wasn't throwing it away; Dwight said it was a perfect pass, any lower and [cornerback Everson] Walls would have batted it away—but it sure wasn't The Pass."

Whatever. No matter what it is called, the play has become a major part of football history. Perhaps more than any other single play in his long career, The Catch made Joe Montana an enduring figure in sports. Writer Dick Schaap commented, "It was, in a very real sense, the play that spawned the legend of Joe Montana."

It was also a pivotal moment in 49ers history. Afterward, the team would go on to become the dominant force in football for a decade, winning four Super Bowls in nine seasons and making the playoffs eight out of the next 10 years.

ON TO THE SUPER BOWL

Before that long string of triumphs could happen, however, it was on to the team's first Super Bowl appearance—arguably the most important contest in San Francisco's history. That game, Super Bowl XVI, took place against the Cincinnati Bengals on January 24, 1982, in the Silverdome in Pontiac, Michigan (a suburb of Detroit).

Led by Montana, and watched by an estimated 85 million television viewers, the 49ers played magnificently. By halftime, they had a 20-0 lead. Although the Bengals rallied in the second half, the 49ers continued to dominate and won the game 26-21. It was a triumph not only for the team but also for its star quarterback: Montana was voted the game's MVP, having completed 14 of 22 passes for 157 yards and one touchdown, while also rushing for 18 yards and a touchdown on the ground.

To say the least, the 1981 season had been a good one for Montana. He had led the 49ers in one of the most dramatic turnarounds in NFL history, as the team emerged from a string of losing seasons to achieve victory in the Super Bowl. The quarterback commented, "Of all my years in pro football, that had to be one of the best. Winning something for the first time, particularly like we did, coming from the absolute bottom, changes the whole team, changes everyone's outlook."

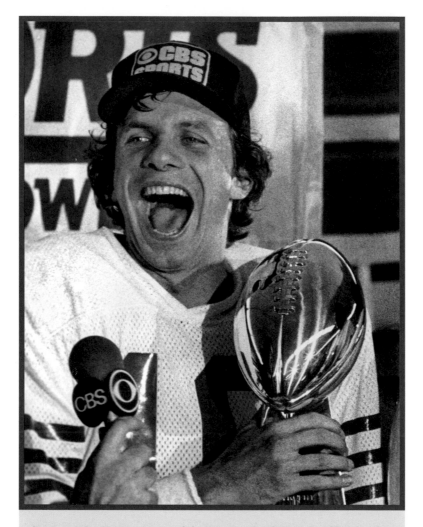

An ecstatic Joe Montana grasped the Vince Lombardi Super Bowl Trophy after the 49ers beat the Bengals, 26-21, to win their first championship. About the victory in Super Bowl XVI, Montana said, "Winning something for the first time, particularly like we did, coming from the absolute bottom, changes the whole team, changes everyone's outlook."

1982–1983: GOOD, BUT NOT GOOD ENOUGH

A great feeling was not Montana's only prize that year. The quarterback was rewarded financially as well. He accepted a four-year contract with the 49ers worth more than

$1.7 million, and he signed up for a number of profitable product endorsement deals during the off-season.

Unfortunately, the 1982 season proved to be disappointing. It was shortened by a players' strike that lasted for 57 days, so the 49ers played only nine games. Montana did well enough, passing for 2,613 yards in those nine games and breaking the 300-yard mark in five straight games. But the team as a unit did not do well. It lost six games, including all five at home.

The next season was an improvement. The 49ers finished with a 10–6 record (winning the final three games of the season) to earn their second NFC West Division title in three years. Once again, Montana led this rebound with another excellent personal record, passing for 3,910 yards and connecting on 26 touchdowns.

"JOE'S THE GUY"

49ers owner Eddie DeBartolo has this to say, in a *San Francisco Chronicle* article, about Joe Montana's role in shaping the powerhouse team of the 1980s:

Without question, he's the guy who started it all. He's the guy who made things happen. We had Bill [Walsh]. Joe came along with [Dwight] Clark. Dwight did a lot of amazing things. [But] Joe's the guy, he's the mixer, that made it all work. If he was not there, I think there would be a different legacy for the 49ers. He really put the franchise on the map. I won't say he did it single-handedly. We had some players, but we didn't have a lot of great players back then. His mystique and his leadership and Bill Walsh and his system, it all led to what it is and what he created.

In the divisional playoffs, the 49ers hosted the Detroit Lions at Candlestick Park. The 49ers led early on and were ahead 17-9 as the final quarter began. The Lions scored two touchdowns to take the lead, 23-17, with five minutes left—which meant it was time for another Montana comeback. He completed six passes, including hitting Freddie Solomon for a game-winning, 14-yard touchdown pass with 1:23 left. The touchdown put the 49ers ahead 24-23; when a field-goal attempt by Lions kicker Eddie Murray missed, the game was over.

The next week, the 49ers experienced still another thrilling comeback that was good—but not good enough. It happened during the NFC Championship Game at RFK Stadium against the Washington Redskins. Despite being down 21-0 heading into the fourth quarter, the 49ers managed to tie the game—thanks, in part, to a 23-yard touchdown pass from Montana to wide receiver Mike Wilson and a 76-yard touchdown pass from Montana to Freddie Solomon.

Unfortunately for San Francisco, a field goal by Redskin Mark Moseley won the game for Washington, 24-21. The 49ers' hopes for an appearance in Super Bowl XVIII were dashed.

ANOTHER SUPER BOWL TRIP

After these two heartbreaking seasons, the 49ers came back in 1984 as very strong contenders. In fact, 1984 was one of the best years in San Francisco's history. The team finished the regular season with a 15–1 record. In nearly every one of these games, the 49ers prevailed from the start; they had to come from behind in the fourth quarter on only two occasions.

In the playoffs, the 49ers beat the New York Giants, 21-10, and the Chicago Bears, 23-0, to earn a spot in Super Bowl XIX, which was played on January 20, 1985, against the Miami Dolphins. An estimated 116 million viewers watched the contest on television.

In Super Bowl XIX, Joe Montana scampered for a touchdown against the Miami Dolphins. Besides his rushing score, Montana also threw for three touchdowns as San Francisco won 38-16. For the second time, he was named the MVP of the Super Bowl.

Montana was eagerly looking forward to the game. First of all, it was being held at Stanford Stadium, on the campus of Stanford University near San Francisco. Montana loved being able to play so close to home. He also relished the prospect of facing Miami's great quarterback, Dan Marino—and defeating him.

Miami took an early lead in the game, but the 49ers soon succeeded in overcoming it. They also succeeded in shutting down Marino's passing game. San Francisco began to dominate in the second quarter and never let up. The 49ers limited Miami to 314 yards and just 25 rushing yards for the entire contest. In the end, the Dolphins went down 38-16, and the 49ers had their second Super Bowl victory.

San Francisco set a Super Bowl record that year with 537 yards, breaking the former record of 429 yards set by the Oakland Raiders in Super Bowl XI. San Francisco's final score, 38 points, tied another Super Bowl record, set by the Raiders in Super Bowl XVIII.

Personally, Montana had a superb game. He completed 24 of 35 passes, setting a Super Bowl record of 331 passing yards for three touchdowns. He also had five rushes for 59 yards and one rushing touchdown—the most rushing yards ever gained by a quarterback in the Super Bowl. For this stellar performance, Montana was voted Super Bowl MVP for the second time. *The New York Times* commented, "Montana was, at times, a magician. He . . . executed his plays magnificently."

"THANK GOD, THEY GOT SOMEBODY TALL ENOUGH"

As 1985 continued, it was a memorable year for Montana in his personal life as well; he married for a third time. Montana had been a bachelor for a couple of years after his first marriage before he married again, to an airline stewardess named Cass Castillo. He and Cass had met in 1979 and married in 1981, but were divorced in 1984.

Later that year, he met an actress named Jennifer Wallace. They both had been hired to appear in a Schick razor commercial that had a theme of "Wanted: Joe Montana." Jennifer played the role of the Schick Sheriff, who always got her man—a cowboy played, of course, by Montana. Jennifer liked her costar immediately, if only because of his height; the six-foot-tall actress recalled, "My first impression of Joe was, 'Thank God, they got somebody tall enough.' The two men I had worked with before had to stand on apple crates."

Joe Montana met actress Jennifer Wallace in 1984 while they were filming a Schick television commercial. They were married a year later. Here, the couple is seen at Giants Stadium before the 1986 NFC divisional playoff game between the 49ers and the New York Giants.

Joe was strongly attracted to her as well. He was nervous, however, while the commercial was being shot, which was unusual for someone known for his cool under pressure. Montana recalled that the director told Jennifer to calm him down—so she pinched him on the rear.

Shooting the commercial took two days, and by the end, Montana worked up enough courage to ask Wallace out. They began to date regularly, the relationship quickly became serious, and Montana proposed. He took Wallace to his favorite park in San Francisco, the Marina Green, and told her to look up. An airplane was flying above them with a streamer reading, "Jen, will you marry me?" He later called this gambit "the riskiest play I ever called." Wallace was looking the wrong way at first, but Montana turned her around; she looked up, saw the plane, and said yes.

The couple wed in 1985. "Marrying Jennifer would have been the highlight of any year," Montana reflected. "She made my life complete." In some ways, though, life was just beginning for him.

The Late 49ers and Kansas City Years

J oe Montana started training camp for the 1985 season with some uncertainty. He had worrisome lower back pain. The problem responded well to treatment, but Montana was not yet at 100 percent by the start of the season.

This no doubt contributed to the 49ers' loss of four of their first seven games. Even after Montana was back at full strength, the team was mediocre for the rest of the season, and the 49ers ended 10–6. The team managed to make the playoffs as a **wild card** but was knocked out in the first round by the New York Giants, 17-3.

A SERIOUS INJURY

Montana had other worries during the 1985 season. In the midst of an era when sports stars were often linked to drug

Whenever he started to get down, he says, he drew inspiration from his wife. Jennifer pushed him to maintain a rigorous program of intense, daily physical therapy. She told him, "*I don't care if you don't play football again, but if you don't, you're not going to get out of this.*"

And so Montana—never a quitter—kept at it. He commented, "I never worked so hard in my life. It was unbelievable."

The therapy, aided by Montana's overall excellent physical condition, quickly paid off. A mere two months after the surgery he was back on the field, starting in a game against the St. Louis Cardinals.

Before his surgery, Montana had missed only two games in his entire pro career because of injury. While recuperating, he had missed eight. During this period, Jeff Kemp filled in as the 49ers' starting quarterback.

The team's record during these months, September and October of '86, was a disappointing 4–3–1. As soon as Montana was back, however, the 49ers caught fire. They won five of their last seven regular-season games and clinched the NFC West title.

Unfortunately, New York then stomped them in the playoffs, 49-3. To make matters worse, Montana was injured again when he collided with the Giants' nose tackle, Jim Burt, and suffered a mild concussion. Montana saw double and had a headache for a little while, but a brain scan showed no serious injury.

A BACKUP FOR JOE COOL

The 1987 season was a shortened one because of a 24-day players' strike. Teams only played 15 games instead of 16 because of the strike, and replacement players filled the rosters for three games during the walkout. The 49ers had another good season and had the best record in the league (13–2), but they fell to the Minnesota Vikings at home in the playoffs, 36-24. This was the third year in a row that San Francisco had made the playoffs only to lose in the first round.

Perhaps the major event affecting Montana that year came in April, when the 49ers acquired Steve Young, a promising player who had started with Tampa Bay, as a backup for him. The two men never became close, though they respected each other's abilities and maintained a healthy competition. Montana said in 1988, "We're friends, Steve and I. But out on the practice field, if he doesn't hate me as much as I hate him, then there's something wrong."

Montana admits that the 49ers were smart to look for an eventual replacement for him. After all, he was in his early 30s and the condition of his back was uncertain. Montana, however, was not yet ready to be replaced, and he proved it on the field. In the 1987 season, with Montana still the starter, the team lost only two games, and late in the year he completed 22 passes in a row—an NFL record.

Unfortunately, Montana injured himself again the week after setting that record, this time hurting his left **hamstring**. He played only sparingly for the rest of the 1987 season. Montana continued to suffer an increasing number of injuries during 1988 and 1989 to his back, elbow, knee, and ribs, but he was never out for more than a week or two at a time.

ON TO A THIRD SUPER BOWL

In the 1988 season's first game, Montana injured his elbow while leading the team to a victory over the New Orleans Saints. Steve Young stepped in as the starting quarterback for the next game, but he performed poorly. After that, with Montana off and on the injured list, Young occasionally filled in as the starter—during the season, Montana started 13 games, Young started three.

The team lost five of its first 11 games and finished the season at 10–6. Only a strong finish kept San Francisco from missing the playoffs. The team was not heavily favored going into the postseason, but the 49ers upset all the predictions of failure.

First, the 49ers took revenge on the Minnesota Vikings, paying them back for the previous year's humiliation by thrashing them 34-9 in the first round. Then, in Chicago, the 49ers stomped the Bears 28-3 in subzero weather. This victory made the 49ers the first team to win an NFC Championship Game on the road since 1979.

Montana had played well despite his nagging injuries. During the 1988 regular season, he had 238 completions for 2,981 yards and 18 touchdowns. He added 132 rushing yards. The quarterback also played well in the postseason, throwing for 466 yards and six touchdowns, with only one interception, in the two NFC playoff games.

Thanks to its victory over Chicago, San Francisco was making its third trip to the Super Bowl. This was Super Bowl XXIII, played in Miami on January 22, 1989, against the Cincinnati Bengals—the second championship meeting between the two teams.

BREAKING THE TENSION

The first three quarters of the game were fairly uneventful, and at halftime it was tied 3-3—the first halftime tie in Super Bowl history. The two teams traded field goals and touchdowns in the second half, and Cincinnati went ahead, 16-13, with a field goal late in the fourth quarter. With only 3:20 on the clock, San Francisco had the ball on its own 8-yard line.

Then The Comeback Kid made another appearance. From the start, Montana's performance demonstrated how his cool under pressure could help his teammates channel their nervous energy. Montana commented, "Some of the guys seemed more than normally tense, especially Harris Barton, a great offensive tackle who has a tendency to get nervous."

The tension broke when Montana spotted a famous comedian, John Candy, in the stands and casually pointed him out. "Joe said, 'Hey, check it out, there's John Candy,'" Barton recalled. "I looked up and there was John Candy in the stands, eating popcorn. I'm thinking, 'Yeah, wow.'

"Then it's like, 'What the heck am I doing? I've got to get my head in the game.' The ref blew his whistle and Joe said, 'OK, here we go.' He called the play and off we went." Montana's relaxed comment, offhandedly pointing out a celebrity in the crowd, had broken the tension. It let his team focus and concentrate on the job at hand.

"IT TOOK EVERYTHING I HAD"

The job was a stunning 92-yard march down the field in less than three minutes. Montana recalled, "We just kept the pressure on them. I made sure we got something out of every play. If I had somebody open right away, even if he wasn't my primary receiver, I gave it to him and let him gain five yards. Just so we had something positive on every play."

The pressure was so intense that it nearly got to Joe Cool himself. At one point during the drive, Montana hyperventilated and nearly passed out—a combination, perhaps, of the pressure to win, the heat in Miami, and the fact that he had to yell at the top of his lungs to be heard by the other players. The quarterback said, "It took everything I had." But it was worth the effort: The drive culminated in a winning touchdown pass to John Taylor with only 34 seconds left.

Seen in retrospect, that particular pass might seem like an easy one. Seen from above, Taylor appeared to be wide open. But a camera behind Montana showed that he passed the ball through a narrow space, only a few feet wide, between the cornerback and the safety. This window was open for no more than a fraction of a second, but—great quarterback that he was—Montana found it.

"WAS THERE EVER ANY DOUBT?"

It was, by any benchmark, an amazing performance—but one to be expected of someone like Montana. Sportswriter Leigh

Randy Cross (No. 51) and Joe Montana congratulated wide receiver John Taylor (No. 82) after Taylor grabbed a 10-yard touchdown pass with 34 seconds left in Super Bowl XXIII. Montana had orchestrated yet another fourth-quarter comeback as the 49ers won their third Super Bowl in the 1980s, defeating the Bengals 20-16.

Montville wrote in *Sports Illustrated*, "Was there ever any doubt that he [Montana] simply was going to move those Niners 92 yards down the field in the final 3:20 to beat the Cincinnati Bengals? Of course not. He completed one pass, and then another, and another. Eight of nine passes during the drive. Was there ever any better high-pressure bit of football business?"

Montana's mother also commented on the thrill of that long drive. Theresa Montana told a reporter, "When they started the last drive, do you know what I was thinking? . . . The 1979 Cotton Bowl, when he brought Notre Dame from behind in the fourth quarter. That was the best—until now."

Wide receiver Jerry Rice was named the game's MVP; he had caught 11 of the 23 completed passes Montana threw, for a total of 215 yards, setting a Super Bowl record. Montana had also played wonderfully—those 23 completions (out of 36 attempts) set another Super Bowl record, of 357 yards. Montana also threw for two touchdowns and gained 13 rushing yards.

Of all the pro games he ever played, Montana says, this one created one of his fondest memories. The quarterback commented, "Driving a team in the last minute and throwing a touchdown pass to win the Super Bowl—that's the kind of thing you dream about as a kid."

THE GREATEST

Super Bowl XXIII, against the Cincinnati Bengals, brought out the best in the 49ers' star quarterback. In particular, there was that famous final drive. Starting with a three-point deficit and 3:20 left in the game, with the ball on the 49ers' 8-yard line, Joe Montana led a march down the field that culminated in a winning touchdown pass to John Taylor with only 34 seconds left. According to an article on the Pro Football Hall of Fame Web site, 49ers coach Bill Walsh commented:

> That was one of the great drives in football history, and every one of the calls was dependent on Joe exercising his discipline and his decision-making ability. Joe was perfect in every respect. He was physically, mentally, emotionally in control. To watch Joe on that series, you were watching the greatest quarterback of all time.

1989

Super Bowl XXIII marked an important transition in Montana's career. It was the last game for Bill Walsh, the coach who had drafted the quarterback and nurtured his rise to prominence; he retired later that year.

Walsh chose George Seifert, the 49ers' defensive coordinator, to be his successor. Guided by Seifert and Montana, the 49ers had another outstanding season in 1989, ending with a 14–2 record. (The two losses were only by a total of five points.)

1989 was also an excellent year for Montana personally. During the season, Montana had a **passer rating** of 112.4, then the best in NFL history, and he did even better in the playoffs. He completed 78 percent of his passes for 800 yards and 11 touchdowns without a single interception. His season accomplishments nabbed him the league's MVP title, as well as the NFL Offensive Player of the Year award.

The 49ers did not slow up. They stormed through the playoffs, making quick work of the Vikings (41-13) and the Rams (30-3) and cementing a fourth Super Bowl appearance.

Super Bowl XXIV, played on January 28, 1990, at the Superdome in New Orleans, pitted the 49ers against the Denver Broncos. It was another triumphant victory for the 49ers in these, their glory years. San Francisco dominated the game almost from the opening kickoff, and the contest ended with a crushing score of 55-10—the most lopsided score, until then, in Super Bowl history.

Back-to-back Super Bowl victories? Montana simply said, "You can't do much better than that." As for his own performance, the quarterback was nearly flawless. He completed 22 of 29 passes, for 297 yards and a Super Bowl-record five touchdowns. He also earned the game's MVP award for a record third time. Referring to the back injury that had nearly ended Montana's playing days, writer Dick Schaap commented, "Not bad for a guy whose career was supposed to be over four years earlier."

Joe Montana saluted the crowd after the 49ers' 55-10 blowout of the Denver Broncos in Super Bowl XXIV on January 28, 1990. Montana passed for a Super Bowl-record five touchdowns.

ANOTHER OUTSTANDING YEAR

1990 was another outstanding year—perhaps Montana's best year of all, statistically speaking. In the season opener against the New Orleans Saints, he completed four passes for 60 yards on the game's final drive, thus setting up a game-winning field goal. He followed this with four games in which he threw for more than 300 yards.

At the relatively advanced age of 34, in his twelfth year of pro ball and increasingly plagued by injuries, Montana threw more passes and gained more yards than ever before in his career. True, he did miss one game (a strained abdomen kept him out), but he started all the others. Once again, Montana was named the season's MVP, and he also received *Sports Illustrated*'s "Sportsman of the Year" award.

As a team, the 49ers continued to ride high. They won their first 10 games and finished the season 14–2—the best record in the NFL that year. In 1990, the 49ers also set a league record of 18 consecutive road victories, a streak that had begun in 1988.

The team beat the Redskins in the first round of the play-offs, advancing to the NFC Championship Game against the New York Giants. Unfortunately for San Francisco, the Giants won on the last play of the game, a 42-yard field goal, for a score of 15-13.

A BAD HIT

As if that defeat was not enough, Giants defensive end Leonard Marshall delivered a fourth-quarter blind-side sack that Montana says is the hardest hit he ever took. It left him with a concussion, a bruised sternum, a fractured rib, and a broken finger. It was a devastating blow and one that would have far-reaching consequences. Montana commented: "I didn't realize it at the time, but that was, basically, the end of my football career in San Francisco."

Montana recovered, but the injuries kept piling up. During training camp the following summer, Montana developed tendonitis in his right elbow, underwent surgery, and had to miss the entire 1991 season. For the rest of the year, he says, he "just stood on the sidelines and tried to give some good advice to Steve Young."

The elbow injury continued to plague Montana in 1992, and he sat out the first 15 games, watching Young continue to be the team's starting quarterback. It was a difficult time, Montana said: "For any player, it's uncomfortable to stay on the sidelines. If you're comfortable there, you'll always be there."

THE LAST NINERS GAME

Finally, in the last game of the regular season, against Detroit, Montana played in the second half. He knew it was going to be a farewell performance. He had not played for nearly two full

New York Giants defensive end Leonard Marshall sacked Joe Montana during the NFC Championship Game on January 20, 1991. Marshall's hit left Montana with a concussion, a bruised sternum, a fractured rib, and a broken finger. Injuries would hamper Montana for the next two seasons.

seasons, and he also knew that the Niners' staff did not plan to use him in the playoffs. So, he said, "I knew deep inside me that this was the last time I was going to play for the 49ers."

He made it a good one, completing 15 of 21 passes, two of them for touchdowns, and running with the ball three times. After the game, Montana asked to keep a touchdown ball as a souvenir, something he normally did not do. He also said good-bye to his teammates, although they did not believe he would really be gone the following year.

But gone he was. Early in 1993, Seifert made it official: Beginning that fall, Steve Young would be the 49ers' starting quarterback. It was, as many observers pointed out, the end of an era—and the loss to San Francisco of a beloved athlete. Reflecting how closely the quarterback was associated with the city, NBC News anchor Tom Brokaw commented, "San Francisco still will have the Golden Gate Bridge, cable cars, Fisherman's Wharf, North Beach, and the best marriage of city, sea, and sky in America, but it will no longer have Joe Montana."

REVITALIZING THE CHIEFS

Meanwhile, his agent had been negotiating with other teams; Montana knew that the end of his time with the 49ers was near, but he did not want to retire. Both the Kansas City Chiefs and the Arizona Cardinals were interested. The Cardinals offered more money, but the Chiefs offered him a better chance at getting to another Super Bowl. Montana chose the Chiefs, and the

WELCOME TO JOE, MONTANA

At the start of Joe Montana's first season with the Kansas City Chiefs, a publicity stunt centered on him and the tiny town of Ismay, in Custer County in eastern Montana. A Kansas City radio station challenged any small town in Montana to legally rename itself Joe, Montana for the length of the football season.

Ismay, population 26 at the time, accepted the challenge. The residents of the newly renamed ranching community held a July Fourth celebration that attracted more than 2,000 people and earned the town more than $70,000, mostly through the sale of "Joe, Montana" souvenirs. It was enough money to build the town a combination community hall and firehouse.

trade was made in April 1993. Joe and Jennifer and their four children moved to Kansas City in time for training camp.

The Chiefs had been a strong team behind quarterback Len Dawson, but since his retirement in 1975, they had dramatically worsened. In fact, the team at one point had six losing seasons in a row, and it had gone 21 years without winning a postseason game and 23 years without reaching the **American Football Conference** (AFC) Championship Game.

There was cause for hope, however. The Chiefs' coach, Marty Schottenheimer, joined the organization in 1989 and had given them four winning seasons. Kansas City also had a new offensive coordinator, Paul Hackett, who had been Montana's quarterback coach in San Francisco for three years. And the team had two gifted new arrivals: Marcus Allen, a former Raiders running back, and Montana, who wore No. 19 for the Chiefs.

A SHAVING CREAM WELCOME

Even though Montana had spent his entire professional career with one team, he found the transition to a new one fairly easy. For one thing, there were the practical jokes.

Montana had long had a reputation among the Niners as someone who liked to play practical jokes. So, on one of Montana's first practice days with the Chiefs, **defensive back** Bennie Thompson filled Montana's helmet with shaving cream. (Luckily, Montana looked inside before he put it on.) The quarterback immediately felt welcome, he said: "As soon as I saw the shaving cream, I knew I was home."

The teasing atmosphere continued into the team's opening game, against the Tampa Bay Buccaneers. The Bucs' quarterback was Montana's friend and former teammate Steve DeBerg, who had been the Chiefs' starting quarterback for several years. DeBerg left a welcoming present for Montana in his locker before the game: a pair of size-16 shoes. The accompanying note read: "Stop trying to follow in my footsteps."

FIRST GAMES FOR THE CHIEFS

There was some worry about how Montana would perform in that first game. After all, he had only played half of one game in the previous two years. He acquitted himself well, however, completing his first eight passes. The Chiefs won 27-3, and Montana was named the AFC Offensive Player of the Week.

Injuries, though, slowed him again. In the third quarter of that opening game, he sprained his wrist. The following week, in a game against Houston, Schottenheimer started Dave Krieg at quarterback, even though Montana said his wrist felt fine. A few games later, Montana pulled a hamstring.

Montana recovered from that injury and returned after a rest to beat San Diego in a comeback victory, again being named the AFC Offensive Player of the Week. But he strained his hamstring again and was forced to sit out the next three games.

Ten games into the season, the Chiefs were 7–3 and Montana had missed half of them. But he played the last six games of the regular season, as well as the playoff games. For his first game back, against Buffalo, Montana was again named the AFC Offensive Player of the Week, for the third time that season. Unfortunately, he suffered a mild concussion in a December game against San Diego and had to leave the game briefly.

THINKING ABOUT RETIREMENT

The Chiefs ended the regular season 11–5 and won the AFC West Division. For the first playoff game, against the Pittsburgh Steelers, it was so cold at Arrowhead Stadium, the home of the Chiefs, that Montana initially wore gloves. But they made him clumsy—his first seven passes were incomplete—and he stopped wearing them.

Kansas City won that day and advanced to the next round, against the Houston Oilers. Houston took a commanding 10-0 lead in the first quarter, and going into the fourth quarter, the Oilers were still leading, 10-7. It was time for The Comeback

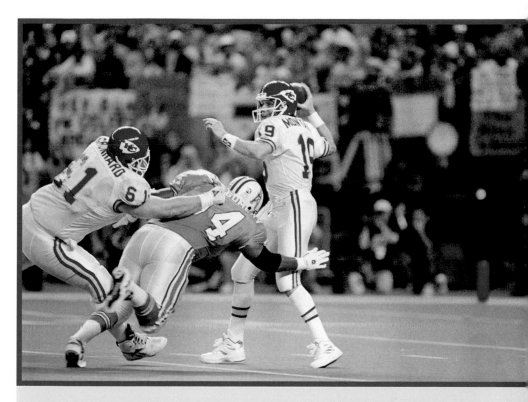

Glenn Montgomery of the Houston Oilers put pressure on Joe Montana as he attempted a pass in the first quarter of an AFC playoff game on January 16, 1994. Montana led three touchdown drives in the last nine minutes of the game to give Kansas City the victory. In his first year with the Chiefs, Montana led Kansas City all the way to the AFC Championship Game.

Kid to do his stuff, and he did. The Chiefs won, scoring three touchdowns in the last nine minutes, including two touchdown passes that Montana threw within a minute of each other.

Then it was on to the AFC Championship Game against Buffalo. Unfortunately, Montana suffered another concussion that day and had to sit out part of the game. The Chiefs lost, 30-13.

It was at this point, Montana says, that he started to think about retirement. "I didn't know how many more concussions I could take," he said. "The people who hit me were getting bigger and stronger and faster every year." However, when Montana was selected for the Pro Bowl that year, any serious thoughts of retirement ended. He started to think instead about leading the Chiefs to the Super Bowl.

WINDING DOWN

During the 1994 season, Montana started in all but two games. The first three were victories, including a battle against the 49ers and Montana's successor there, Steve Young—a game that drew the second-largest crowd in Arrowhead Stadium history.

Before the game, the media heavily built up the Montana-Young rivalry, pitting the older pro against the younger man who had replaced him. Montana publicly dismissed the rivalry and kept his statements as low key as possible, but privately he was eager to match up against Young. After the game, Chiefs defensive end Neil Smith told reporters that it had, indeed, been an important contest for Montana: "Joe never mentioned to us what this game meant to him and what it was all about. But we knew that deep down inside he really wanted it. And so did we."

As it turned out, the game ended in a sweet 24-17 triumph for the Chiefs. Montana was happy to win, of course, although on another level he had also hoped the Niners would do well. He had wanted them to get to the Super Bowl—so that he could face them there.

Alas, Montana's fortunes went downhill as the 1994 season progressed. After the first three victories, the next two games were disasters, without even a single touchdown. Montana suffered the first shutout of his career, as the Chiefs lost 16-0 to the Rams.

Worse, the quarterback was increasingly tired and sore, and he had to admit that, more and more, the game was less fun. He said, "For the first time in my life, football was beginning to feel like a job. It wasn't just that in Kansas City I was lifting weights for the first time in my career, and it wasn't just that our work-days were longer than they were in San Francisco. It was me."

WRAPPING IT UP

In what proved to be the last year of Montana's career, he brought the Chiefs' record to 7–4 before spraining his foot and sitting out the next two games. He was back in time for victories over the Oilers and the Raiders, however, leading the team into the playoffs as a wild card.

Then came his final NFL game: the opening round of the playoffs, against the Miami Dolphins. Despite increasing pain and stiffness, the quarterback played beautifully. *The New York Times* commented, "The day began with a flawless Montana drive, 80 yards in 11 plays with Montana completing 6 passes in 6 attempts and baffling the Dolphin defense with play action that bordered on the sleight of hand when he hit [tight end Derrick] Walker with a 1-yard touchdown pass in the corner of the end zone." Despite this performance, however, the Chiefs lost, 27–17.

And that was it: Joe Montana decided to retire after this game. He did not have to; one more year remained on his con-tract. But he had been a professional football player all his adult life, and he was tired.

Despite his weariness, Montana stayed strong right up to the end of his playing days. Sports broadcaster Pat Haden commented, "He didn't end his career as a backup. He didn't go out with a whimper. He went out with a bang. He raised the level of people around him in Kansas City just as he did in San Francisco."

Retirement

The public outpouring of emotion for Joe Montana was strong. Two public farewell ceremonies were held in 1995, one in San Francisco and one in Kansas City. The event in San Francisco was by far the larger, reflecting the city's long and heartfelt relationship with the athlete. Held outdoors at a public plaza, an estimated 30,000 well-wishers attended to honor Montana. Many of them carried hand-made banners or wore replicas of his famous No. 16 jersey.

Bill Walsh was the master of ceremonies for the event. Another pro football legend, player-coach-commentator John Madden, was among the speakers. Montana himself gave a short speech, although he admitted he was terrified.

He remarked beforehand that he would rather face a **blitz** than speak in front of so many people. Nonetheless, he did

Eddie DeBartolo *(right)*, the owner of the 49ers, sat with Joe Montana as former coaches and teammates applauded during a ceremony in April 1995 to honor Montana after his retirement. An estimated 30,000 fans attended the event, which was held at a public plaza in San Francisco.

well. He thanked everyone for the support he received over the years and commented on how he had assumed he would play forever: "I really, truly never thought this day would ever come where I would say that word—retirement."

There were also several private celebrations to honor his retirement, notably a surprise party organized by Jennifer Montana. On the evening of the party, she and Joe met 49ers owner Eddie DeBartolo and his wife, Candy, for drinks at a hotel in San Francisco, then got into a limousine to go to dinner. Joe thought that they were headed to a DeBartolo family function.

The limo let the group out at the elegant Flood Mansion. (It once was a private home but now serves as a hall for receptions and dinner parties.) It was not until Montana walked in that he realized what was happening.

Dozens of his friends and family were waiting to greet him. Among the well-wishers were Carl Crawley, who had coached Joe in the Monongahela Little Wildcats peewee league; Jeff Petrucci, Joe's high school quarterback coach; Nick DeCicco, his roommate at Notre Dame; former teammates Steve DeBerg, Dave Krieg, and Dwight Clark; and coaches Bill Walsh and George Seifert.

RETIRING NUMBER 16

Two years later, in 1997, the Niners officially retired Montana's jersey number. As in every occasion in which he was in the spotlight, the athlete had somewhat mixed feelings about the official ceremony held for it. He appreciated the honor, but he was always uncomfortable being the center of attention. Before the ceremony, Montana commented in the *San Francisco Chronicle*, "It's going to be a lot of fun, [but] I can't wait till it's over. I hate those kinds of things. I'm very honored they wanted to do it. Everybody keeps saying, 'It's about time.' Well, it wasn't even a necessity for me. I had a great career here. I'm just happy they decided to do it."

The ceremony to retire Montana's number took place during a Niners home game against the Denver Broncos. It was a notable game for several reasons. First of all, San Francisco beat the Broncos, 34-17. Also, Jerry Rice, the 49ers' outstanding wide receiver (and one of Montana's favorites), scored his 1,000th point. But what made the game a really special event was the ceremony centered on No. 16, during which a crowd of 68,461 emotional fans gave the former quarterback a standing ovation.

There were a number of speakers. Among them was Bill Walsh, who praised Montana as "the greatest football player of our time, and possibly of all time." And Eddie DeBartolo compared Montana to a knight of old who rode in to save the day: "When he came to this organization, he came as Sir Lancelot came to Camelot."

For his part, Montana thanked Walsh, DeBartolo, his family, all of his teammates over the years, and "the greatest fans anywhere in the greatest city anywhere." He went on to express amazement at how far he had come: "I'm honored to be standing here tonight. When I came here in 1979, I never imagined I'd be in this position."

MORE HONORS

Many more honors have continued to pour in over the years for Montana. For example, in 1999, the *Sporting News* ranked him third among the "100 Greatest Football Players of All Time." In 2000, his first year of eligibility, he was inducted into the Pro Football Hall of Fame.

In 2004, *Sporting News* ranked Montana second among its "50 Greatest Quarterbacks." In 2006, *Sports Illustrated* named him No. 1 on a list of "Top 10 Clutch Quarterbacks of All Time." According to ESPN's *SportsCentury*, he was No. 25 among the "Greatest Athletes of the 20th Century," and *Sports Illustrated* ranked him twenty-third on its "40 for the Ages" list.

There have been many honors from the world outside pro sports as well. Some of these have come from Montana's hometown of Monongahela. They have been made despite the occcasional resistance in the town to naming things after the athlete. The resistance is due to criticism of Montana among residents of the region. Chief among these criticisms is that Montana has neglected his hometown in the years since his success.

It is true that he seldom returns to the Monongahela Valley from his home near Calistoga, California, in the Napa Valley wine country north of San Francisco. (Montana's parents live nearby, having moved in 1986.) But Montana says

The San Francisco 49ers retired Joe Montana's number—16—on December 15, 1997, during halftime of a game between the 49ers and the Broncos. Montana thanked his family, his teammates, and "the greatest fans anywhere in the greatest city anywhere."

in his defense that he is simply not very interested in times gone by: "It's hard because I don't typically live in my past. I still get a lot of grief . . . in Monongahela because I don't go back there a lot. [But] there are so many things that are happening now, it's hard to live back then."

"THE ULTIMATE FEELING"

Nonetheless, despite any lingering resentment toward Montana in his hometown, a pair of bridges on the Mon-Fayette Expressway has been named for him. Also, in 2006 his old high school, Ringgold High, named its stadium in his honor. The school also inducted him into its first Sports Hall of Fame class, alongside such distinguished Ringgold graduates as Stan Musial and Ken Griffey, Sr.

During the ceremonies at Ringgold High, Montana said that he was deeply honored to be recognized. Being honored in Monongahela was in some ways more meaningful than the Pro Football Hall of Fame, he said, according to the *Pittsburgh Tribune-Review*, "because this [recognition] is from your friends and your family in an area [where] you grew up. When you think about it, that's the ultimate feeling."

On the other hand, Montana also remarked, being inducted into a hall of fame was just another reminder that he was getting old. He said, "It's always scary when you get into a hall of fame. I always tell people it's like the last nail in your coffin."

And there have been other, more unusual honors from outside the world of pro sports. Perhaps the strangest came in 2006, when a rabid football fan in Mississippi persuaded his wife to give their newborn son the first name ESPN (pronounced "Espen"). The family's last name is Real, and the boy's middle name is . . . Montana.

KEEPING BUSY

After years of punishing play on the football field, no one would criticize Montana if he spent the rest of his days relaxing in the sun with a cool drink. In the years since his retirement, however, the athlete has certainly not been idle.

The same drive and restless energy that helped make him a superhero in football have simply been channeled in other directions. Journalist Wright Thompson commented, "Somewhere along the way, he managed to replace one obsession with another. With many more, actually, packing hobbies and jobs and projects into the void."

One activity he has conspicuously *not* pursued is coaching. A number of people have suggested it over the years. Montana, however, says he is simply not interested. He said in one television interview, "I have four children, and I don't want 57 more of them."

But there have been other interests. For a time, he was involved in auto racing, which had first piqued his interest when he took part in a 1984 celebrity race in Long Beach, California. Shortly after his retirement in 1995, Montana became a partner in the Target/Chip Ganassi Racing Team, which races on the Indy Car circuit. The team enjoyed its most successful season that year, which leader Ganassi said was no coincidence: "Joe brought a particular spirit to our team I think we were lacking that certainly put us over the top. He's our quarterback—a natural team leader who keeps everybody very cool."

Montana has focused on other pastimes, too. His interests have included owning and riding Arabian horses, golfing, fishing, practicing martial arts, traveling, and enjoying fine food and wine. Montana also flies his own airplane. He first learned how to pilot a small plane in 1991 and 1992, when injuries forced him to the sidelines. Flying lessons kept him busy during this frustrating time, and in time Jennifer bought him his own single-engine plane.

TV AND MORE

In retirement, Montana has been involved in various publishing and broadcasting ventures. He briefly served as the editor in chief of a football magazine called *In the Redzone.* More successful and more frequent have been his appearances on television sports shows. During his first year of retirement, for example, he was a commentator for NBC Sports during the football season.

More recently, he has been seen on a number of other sports shows, including *Costas Now* and *The Best Damn Sports Show Period.* Once in a while, Montana also shows up on non-sports programs. For example, he appeared in a Billy Ray Cyrus

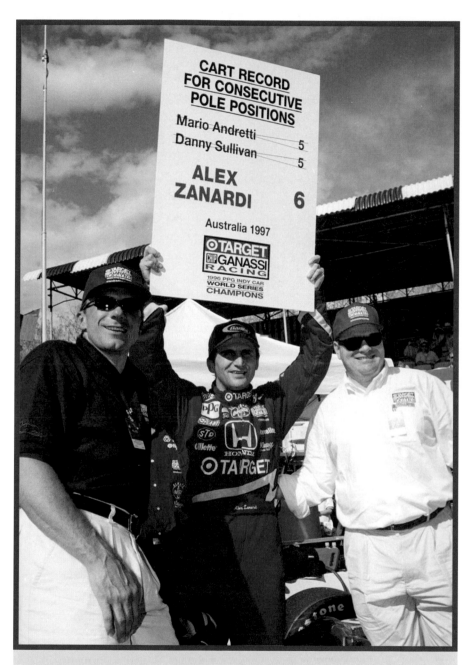

Joe Montana *(left)* celebrated with Indy car driver Alex Zanardi *(center)* and Chip Ganassi after Zanardi had taken his sixth straight pole in April 1997 at the Gold Coast Indy 300 race in Australia. Two years earlier, soon after his retirement, Montana joined Ganassi as a part owner of the Target/Chip Ganassi Racing Team.

concert special called *A Year on the Road*, and in 1987 he co-hosted an episode of *Saturday Night Live*.

But Montana's most prominent appearances on television have been in commercials, as was true during much of his pro career. These ads include spots for Coors beer, Mervyn's department stores, Schick razors, DirecTV, Flexall, Fruit of the Loom, Ford trucks, Disneyland, and Tombstone frozen pizzas.

He has also shot several spots promoting Super Bowl games. For one, he and Ben Roethlisberger, the Pittsburgh Steelers' quarterback, sang a duet of the song "Tomorrow." Montana later commented about this collaboration, "It was ugly. Not a pretty sight."

There is another interesting side note to Montana's film and TV career. Filmmaker Oliver Stone, an avid football fan, wrote the screenplay for the 1983 movie *Scarface*. The lead character, played by Al Pacino, is named Tony Montana in honor of the quarterback.

BUSINESS AND CHARITABLE VENTURES

Montana has also been involved in a number of business ventures over the years. Chief among them was becoming part of the management team at HRJ Capital, a private equity investment firm based in the Bay Area. The company was founded by Montana's former 49ers teammates Ronnie Lott and Harris Barton; the firm changed its name to HRJ (for Harris, Ronnie, and Joe) after Montana joined.

Montana is also a popular motivational speaker and writer. In this capacity, he gives lectures to a wide variety of groups around the country. He is the author or co-author of several motivational books, among them *The Winning Spirit: 16 Timeless Principles That Drive Performance Excellence*.

Still another project has been a wine-producing operation. Montana has long been a wine connoisseur, and he partnered for this venture with a prominent wine maker,

Beringer Vineyards. The wine they produce appears under the label Montagia. Some of the profits from this enterprise go to benefit health facilities in the Napa Valley, the wine region of California where Montana lives.

The athlete is also involved in a number of public service and charity organizations. For example, he learned a few years ago that he suffered from high blood pressure, a life-threatening condition that many Americans face. Since then, he has become a frequent spokesman on the importance of controlling high blood pressure. Another charity he and Jennifer are involved with is the Children's Village of Sonoma County. This organization helps children find stable foster-care homes.

STEPPING BACK FOR FAMILY

For someone as energetic and famous as Joe Montana, there is a real danger in becoming spread too thin and in becoming completely wrapped up in projects. In recent years, Montana has made a strong effort to step back from his many activities to concentrate on his family.

The four Montana children were all less than 10 years old when their father retired. Alexandra was born in 1985, Elizabeth in 1986, Nathaniel in 1989, and Nicholas in 1992. Montana regrets that he missed a good part of his daughters' childhoods, because he was still playing football. "While I was playing, I missed a lot of their growth," he said. "Then I took it for granted that they were always gonna be that size and, next thing you know, they're both out the door."

Alexandra and Elizabeth chose to attend Notre Dame, as Montana did, but his sons are still at home, and he is determined to spend as much time with them as possible. In 2005, his former teammate and longtime friend Ronnie Lott commented, "The last two years have been a wake-up call for him. A wake-up call to be around his boys, to have fun, to be a great dad, to be like his dad was to him."

"THE REAL MEANING OF LIFE"

Montana has never pushed his kids to be athletes, although he enjoys watching them play sports. Montana has also emphasized to them the powerful connection he sees between sports and everyday life, feeling that the lessons learned in one will help the other. He commented, in the book *Montana*:

> Sports has been very good to me. I've been very fortunate in terms of where I am and how I got here. Growing

TOO MUCH FUN

Inevitably, even a superb athlete like Joe Montana slows down. In 2005, he underwent spinal fusion surgery and continues to have problems with one knee that may require a knee-replacement operation. Such physical problems are, of course, a legacy of his rough years on the field. Montana tries to look at it philosophically, however, as he said in a 2007 interview with the *Pittsburgh Tribune-Review*:

> The knee's probably the biggest problem right now, mainly because I have two boys who are active in sports right now, and I want to go beat up on 'em a little bit, but I can't have any fun because my knee won't allow me to.
>
> Other than that, you learn to live with certain things. It becomes part of your life. Unfortunately, we have to live with it. It was easier when you were playing, because there was always something else to look forward to—games—but when that's not there any longer, you see it limits you in what your life can be. But, you know, I chose to play the game, so I'm not complaining about that part of it. But those are things you don't think about when you're playing, because it's just too much fun.

up around sports, you learn how to deal with people in day-to-day life. There are certain rules to life, as there are to games, that put you in the position of learning that it's not my turn, it's his turn, and that in order to succeed we need to work together. These are valuable lessons.

The support that Jennifer's mom and my parents have given us throughout our lives has been instrumental in our success. If Jennifer and I can pass on these lessons and provide half that support to our kids, I'd be very happy. You just hope that you give them a strong foundation, and one hopes that with the way things are going in the real world today, that we never, ever lose touch with who really gives support and where the real meaning of life comes from, and that's your family.

CONTROVERSY

Montana's life in retirement has not been entirely without controversy. For example, in 1995, he unsuccessfully sued a newspaper, the *San Jose Mercury News*, to stop selling posters showing him in a Super Bowl appearance. The case got as far as the California Supreme Court, but the court ruled against Montana. He had to pay the *Mercury News* more than $20,000 in lawyers' fees and court costs.

Montana was in the news again in 2006, when he was absent from a Super Bowl XL pregame show that featured Super Bowl MVPs from past years. The *San Francisco Chronicle* reported that the alleged reason for Montana's absence was that he had insisted on a $100,000 fee, which the NFL had refused to pay. These rumors were untrue, Montana says; he chose instead to attend his son's basketball game and then watch the Super Bowl with his family.

In a radio interview at the time, Montana commented bluntly about the incident. He resented the idea that a former player had to blindly do whatever the league asked him to do. He remarked:

They just can't live with the fact that I don't have to have the NFL to live. They want you to do something, and they expect everyone to say yes and jump. But I have two boys that I have a responsibility to and I enjoy being around. And if I want to go home and watch the game with them, I should have every right.

I don't have to do what the NFL wants me to do. They're putting on a show. And because you don't want to be a part of their show, they get upset, and they have a reporter in the Bay Area, who knows me very well, write a story without even trying to contact me and get my side of the story. It's typical.

"I'VE ALWAYS BEEN AT MY BEST IN THE FOURTH QUARTER"

Such incidents of controversy, fortunately, have been rare during Montana's retirement. As he did while he was playing,

"HE IS DECENCY REWARDED"

In this passage, *Sports Illustrated* writer Rick Teland comments on the legacy of Joe Montana:

You can't root against Joe Montana, even when he's playing against your team. He is decency rewarded, a guy who has paid his dues. He was once the seventh-string quarterback at Notre Dame. Eighty-one players were taken before him in the 1979 NFL Draft. But Montana has never been one to brood. He simply puts it all aside—everything—when he trots onto the field, to the place where he was meant to be, where he's the best there ever was.

During a 2006 visit to the Hartford Fire Department Training Academy in Connecticut, Joe Montana passed an autographed football to a fan. At the event, he spoke about life after football and staying fit. Montana has been quite active since his retirement from the NFL, pursuing his many interests, but he devotes most of his time to his family.

he appears to be having an active, happy, and contented time. He keeps busy, spends time with his family, has fun with it all, and—in most respects—does not seem to miss playing pro ball.

Nonetheless, Montana admits that he misses certain aspects of pro football. "The game was never the same [each week]," he told the *San Francisco Chronicle*. "Very rarely do you have the same things happen to you week after week in a game. It was that thrill of the unknown, and that excitement of you don't know what the score was going to be. I enjoyed that part of it." This excitement, bolstered by the new sense of competition that each game brought, is what he misses most, because, he says, "it's almost impossible to find that anywhere."

In his retirement, as he has been all his life, Montana remains an intensely private person, carefully guarding himself and his family from the glare of the spotlight. Montana has never been comfortable in the public eye; in fact, Jennifer Montana says, her husband treasures his family, in part, because he is not a celebrity to them. She commented, in a *Sports Illustrated* article, "What makes him comfortable is his home and his kids and everyday life, not being put on a pedestal, not being called a hero every five minutes."

One reason Montana avoids the spotlight is that—while being a superstar has many obvious advantages—he has lost his ability to move in public as a normal person. He commented, "I love to eat out, but it's just no fun anymore. There's always a group of people coming by your table, always some guy just pulling up a chair and lighting a cigarette and starting to talk football."

Still, despite such inconveniences, Montana seems to have retained a healthy perspective on life, grateful for the luck he has had and the benefits he has enjoyed. He said, "I've gone places, done things I couldn't have dreamed about when I was growing up in Monongahela. And my life's a long way from being over. It's not even the end of the first half, and remember, I've always been at my best in the fourth quarter."

JOE MONTANA
POSITION: Quarterback

FULL NAME:
Joseph Clifford Montana, Jr.
BORN: June 11, 1956,
New Eagle, Pennsylvania
HEIGHT: 6'2"
WEIGHT: 205 lbs.

COLLEGE:
Notre Dame
TEAMS: San
Francisco 49ers
(1979–1992); Kansas
City Chiefs (1993–1994)

YEAR	TEAM	G	COMP	ATT	PCT	YD	Y/A	TD	INT
1979	SF	16	13	23	56.5	96	4.2	1	0
1980	SF	15	176	273	64.5	1,795	6.6	15	9
1981	SF	16	311	488	63.7	3,565	7.3	19	12
1982	SF	9	213	346	61.6	2,613	7.6	17	11
1983	SF	16	332	515	64.5	3,910	7.6	26	12
1984	SF	16	279	432	64.6	3,630	8.4	28	10
1985	SF	15	303	494	61.3	3,653	7.4	27	13
1986	SF	8	191	307	62.2	2,236	7.3	8	9
1987	SF	13	266	398	66.8	3,054	7.7	31	13
1988	SF	14	238	397	59.9	2,981	7.5	18	10
1989	SF	13	271	386	70.2	3,521	9.1	26	8
1990	SF	15	321	520	61.7	3,944	7.6	26	16
1991	SF	0	OUT FOR SEASON WITH INJURY						
1992	SF	1	15	21	71.4	126	6.0	2	0
1993	KC	11	181	298	60.7	2,144	7.2	13	7
1994	KC	14	299	493	60.6	3,283	6.7	16	9
TOTALS		192	3,409	5,391	63.2	40,551	7.5	273	139

CHRONOLOGY

1956 **June 11** Joseph Clifford Montana, Jr., is born in New Eagle, Pennsylvania; grows up in nearby Monongahela.

1974 Graduates from Ringgold High; named to the *Parade* All-American team.
Wins football scholarship to the University of Notre Dame in South Bend, Indiana.

1977 Becomes the starting quarterback for the Notre Dame Fighting Irish.

1978 Leads Notre Dame to victory over the University of Texas, 38-10, in the Cotton Bowl; Fighting Irish win the national championship.

TIMELINE

1956
Born on June 11 in New Eagle, Pennsylvania

1979
Engineers stunning comeback victory in the Cotton Bowl; is drafted by the 49ers

1982
Leads the 49ers to victory in their first Super Bowl

1956

1985

1977
Becomes the starting quarterback for Notre Dame

1985
The 49ers win their second Super Bowl, 38-16, over Miami

1979   Turns in another stunning performance at the Cotton
        Bowl, scoring a come-from-behind victory over the
        University of Houston, 35-34.
        Graduates from Notre Dame and moves to California.
        Drafted in the third round by the San Francisco 49ers.

1982   **January 10** Leads 49ers in an amazing comeback
        victory over Dallas; the win, which clinched the NFC
        championship, includes the famous play known as
        "The Catch."
        January 24 Leads the 49ers to victory over the Cincinnati
        Bengals, 26-21, in their first Super Bowl; is voted the
        Super Bowl MVP.

1990
Wins third Super
Bowl MVP, as San
Francisco crushes
Denver, 55-10

1994
Retires from
football after two
seasons with the
Kansas City Chiefs

1989   2000

1989
Rallies San
Francisco to beat
Bengals, 20-16,
in Super Bowl

1992
Plays final
game with San
Francisco

2000
Inducted in the
Pro Football
Hall of Fame

JOE MONTANA

1984   The 49ers have one of the best years in their history, finishing 15–1 in the regular season.

1985   **January 20** The 49ers win their second Super Bowl, 38-16, against the Miami Dolphins; Montana is again voted the Super Bowl MVP.
Marries his third wife, Jennifer Wallace; their first child, Alexandra, is born, followed by Elizabeth (1986), Nathaniel (1989), and Nicholas (1992).

1986   Seriously injures his back and undergoes surgery but returns after two months.

1989   **January 22** Leads team to third Super Bowl victory, beating the Cincinnati Bengals, 20-16, with a come-from-behind win.
49ers coach Bill Walsh, who drafted and nurtured Montana, retires and is replaced by George Seifert.
Named MVP of the NFL for the 1989 season.

1990   **January 28** San Francisco makes its fourth Super Bowl appearance; Montana leads the team to a crushing victory over Denver, 55-10, and is named the Super Bowl MVP for the third time.
Named MVP of the NFL for the 1990 season.

1992   Plagued by increasing injuries, plays final game with San Francisco.

1993   Traded to the Kansas City Chiefs; leads them to the AFC Championship Game in his first season.

1994   Retires from football at the end of his second season in Kansas City.

1997   San Francisco retires his jersey, No. 16.

2000   Inducted into the Pro Football Hall of Fame.

GLOSSARY

American Football Conference (AFC)   One of the two conferences in the National Football League (NFL). The AFC was established after the NFL merged with the American Football League (AFL) in 1970.

blitz   A defensive maneuver in which one or more linebackers or defensive backs, who normally remain behind the line of scrimmage, instead charge into the opponents' backfield.

bootleg   An offensive play in which the quarterback fakes a handoff to a running back going one direction while the quarterback goes in the opposite direction to run or pass.

center   A player position on offense. The center snaps the ball.

cornerback   A defensive back who lines up near the line of scrimmage across from a wide receiver. The cornerback's primary job is to disrupt passing routes and to defend against short and medium passes in the passing game and to contain the rusher on rushing plays.

defensive back   A cornerback or safety position on the defensive team; commonly defends against wide receivers on passing plays. Generally there are four defensive backs playing at a time.

disk   The plate of fibrocartilage found between adjacent vertebrae of the spinal column.

draft   The selection of collegiate players for entrance into the National Football League. Typically, the team with the worst record over the previous season picks first in the draft.

end zone   The area between the end line and the goal line, bounded by the sidelines.

extra point   After a touchdown, the scoring team is allowed to add another point by kicking the football through the uprights of the goalpost.

field goal   A scoring play of three points made by kicking the ball through the goalposts in the opponent's end zone.

first down   The first of a set of four downs. Usually, a team that has a first down needs to advance the ball 10 yards to receive another first down, but penalties or field position (i.e. less than 10 yards from the opposing end zone) can affect this.

free safety   A defensive player who lines up the deepest in the secondary and defends the deep middle of the field against the pass.

fourth down   The final of a set of four downs. Unless a first down is achieved or a penalty forces a replay of the down, the team will lose control of the ball after this play. If a team does not think it can get a first down, it will often punt on fourth down or attempt a field goal if close enough to do so.

fullback   A player position on offense. In modern formations this position may be varied, and this player has more blocking responsibilities in comparison to the halfback or tailback.

fumble   When any offensive player loses possession of the ball before the play is blown dead.

goal line   The front of the end zone.

hamstring   Any of three muscles at the back of the thigh that function to flex and rotate the leg and extend the thigh.

interception   A pass that is caught by a defensive player, giving his team the ball.

National Football Conference (NFC)   One of the two conferences in the National Football League (NFL). The NFC was established after the NFL merged with the American Football League (AFL) in 1970.

noseguard   The defensive lineman who lines up opposite the offensive center.

offensive linemen   The offensive players who line up on the line of scrimmage. Their primary job is to block the defensive players.

passer rating   (also quarterback rating) A numeric value used to measure the performance of quarterbacks. It was formulated in 1973, and it uses the player's completion percentage, passing yards, touchdowns, and interceptions.

placekicker   The player who kicks the ball on kickoffs, field-goal attempts, and extra-point attempts.

quarterback   The offensive player who receives the ball from the center at the start of each play. The quarterback will hand off the ball, pass the ball, or run it himself.

redshirt   A college player who skips a year of play without losing a year of eligibility. College athletes are only eligible to play for four years. A player will often redshirt because of an injury or an academic problem.

reverse   A play in which the running back receives a handoff from the quarterback and then runs laterally behind the line of scrimmage before handing off to a receiver running in the opposite direction.

rookie   A player in his first year as a professional.

sack   A tackle of the quarterback behind the line of scrimmage.

tight end   A player position on offense, who lines up on the line of scrimmage next to the offensive tackle. Tight ends are used as blockers during running plays and either run a route or stay in to block during passing plays.

touchdown   A play worth six points in which any part of the ball while legally in the possession of a player crosses the plane of the opponent's goal line. A touchdown allows the team a chance for one extra point by kicking the ball or two points by attempting a two-point conversion.

two-point conversion   A scoring play immediately after a touchdown during which a team can add two points to the score instead of kicking for just one point; in a two-point conversion, the scoring team has one play to run or pass the ball into the end zone from the opponent's 3-yard line in college football and 2-yard line in the NFL.

West Coast offense   An offensive philosophy that uses short, high-percentage passes as the core of a ball-control offense.

wide receiver   A player position on offense. The wide receiver is split wide (usually about 10 yards) from the formation and plays on the line of scrimmage as a split end or one yard off as a flanker.

wild card   The two playoff spots given to the two non-division-winning teams that have the best records in the conference.

yard   One yard of linear distance in the direction of one of the two goals. A field is 100 yards. Typically, a team is required to advance at least 10 yards in order to get a new set of downs.

BIBLIOGRAPHY

Callahan, Tom. "Perfect Timing, Joe." *Time*, January 25, 1982.

Inman, Cam. "25 Years Ago, a No. 82 Pick Turned Golden." *Contra Costa Times*, April 22, 2004.

Montana, Joe, with Richard Weiner. *Joe Montana's The Art and Magic of Quarterbacking*. New York: Henry Holt, 1997.

Montana, Joe, and Dick Schaap. *Montana*. Atlanta: Turner Publishing, 1995.

Montana, Joe, and Tom Mitchell. *The Winning Spirit: 16 Timeless Principles That Drive Performance Excellence*. New York: Random House, 2005.

Plaschke, Bill. "The Bottom Line: Centers React to Quarterback Joe Montana's Retirement." *Sporting News*, April 24, 1995.

Zimmerman, Paul. "The Ultimate Winner." *Sports Illustrated*. August 13, 1990.

FURTHER READING

BOOKS

Barber, Phil. *We Were Champions: The 49ers' Dynasty in Their Own Words*. Chicago: Triumph Books, 2002.

Georgatos, Dennis. *Game of My Life—San Francisco 49ers: Memorable Stories of 49ers Football*. Champaign, Illinois: Sports Publishing LLC, 2007.

Kavanagh, Jack, *Sports Great: Joe Montana*. Hillside, New Jersey: Enslow Publishers, 1992.

Ramen, Fred, *Football Hall of Famers: Joe Montana*. New York: Rosen, 2002.

Sporting News. Pro Football's Greatest Quarterbacks. New York: Sporting News, 2005.

WEB SITES

Joe Montana: A Special Tribute
http://www.sfgate.com/sports/49ers/pages/1997/montana.shtml

The Official Athletic Site of the University of Notre Dame
http://und.cstv.com

Official Site of the National Football League
http://www.nfl.com/

Official Site of the San Francisco 49ers
http://www.sf49ers.com

Pro Football Hall of Fame: Joe Montana
http://www.profootballhof.com/hof/member.jsp?player_id=154

Pro Football Reference
http://www.pro-football-reference.com

PICTURE CREDITS

INDEX

ABOUT THE AUTHOR

ADAM WOOG has written nearly 60 books for adults, young adults, and children. He has a special interest in biography. He lives with his family in Seattle, Washington, where he cheers for his daughter's high school varsity basketball team.